Procreation Is

-The Case for Voluntary Human Extinction

by Anti Procreation

If destruction is violence, creation, too, is violence. Procreation, therefore, involves violence. The creation of what is bound to perish certainly involves violence.

-Mahatma Gandhi

The Anti-natalist Manifesto[1]

We were forcefully brought into existence even though we weren't asked to be born, nor consented thereto. This is unsolicited. Our parents brought us into existence knowing that every human dies very well, without a shadow of guilt. How can't be procreation with knowledge it would lead to death sooner or later, well within 130 years murder?[2] Even if we choose not to call it murder, it's because it's more heinous crime, not less heinous crime than murder. Murder only make death happen a few decades earlier of somebody who was condemned to death by procreation; whereas procreation condemns nonexistent person to life and death, making the victim suffer up to about 120 years and die.[3] If murder is a

---

[1] This manifesto have been published on Reddit /r/antinatalism and Amazon Kindle Store under the pen name 'antiprocreation', I edited a little bit for this book

[2] https://answers.yahoo.com/question/index?qid=20070815053516AAwtavs

[3] Crisp, Quentin S, ANTINATALISM: A THOUGHT EXPERIMENT, Living In The Future, Issue 2, http://www.litfmag.net/issue-2/anti-natalism-a-thought-experiment/

crime, procreation is a sin.[4] The consequence of every procreation is fatal and tragic.[5] Every maternity ward is a crematorium.[6]

Lack of capacity to give consent do not mean somebody can inflict any action to the person that lacks the capacity to give informed consent. For example, minor under age of consent deemed to lack the capacity to give consent, so any sexual contact with such minor is deemed rape unconditionally (statutory rape). Even though for example, medical treatment, vaccination, and compulsory education are inflicted without the informed consent of the child, such action is deemed to be (whether real or purported) best interest of the child to be justifiable. For procreation, the child neither given consent thereto nor have any interest to come into existence, although once came into existence, the child may have the interest to continue their existence.

---

[4] Existential Depression, Facebook Page https://www.facebook.com/permalink.php?id=229835853787959&story_fbid=334158626689014

[5] I was inspired by a warning sign at the Golden Gate Bridge, San Francisco

[6] Watts, Alan W. http://www.goodreads.com/quotes/164339-i-am-what-happens-between-the-maternity-ward-and-the, Perry, Sarah, Every Cradle is a Grave, 2014

Life is indeed life imprisonment without eligibility for parole, followed by the death penalty.[7] Even if we are natural born citizen of our country of citizenship, our stay is only allowed temporarily, we can get deported from the cosmos at any time, condemned to death and executed for illegal immigration. Nobody on the planet allowed to stay for more than 130 years, everybody was deported, i.e. executed before she becomes 130 years old.

Article 2, Paragraph 2 of the Charter of Fundamental Rights of the European Union stipulates that "No one shall be condemned to the death penalty, or executed.". How can't be every procreation a condemnation to death? How can't be every death an execution? There's no intrinsic reason to think that procreation is not a violation of the right to life.

Death is the end of everything, an annihilation; that's all. If we are already condemned to life, we can continue to live without suiciding. But why breed to only endure excruciating torment for decades and die? Breed to exploit as companion human animal? Breed to provide a sibling? Breed to exploit as an insurance and pension for old age? Breed as an investment? Breed to perpetuate genes and last name? Breed to brainwash your religion or ideology? Breed to perpetuate tribe, nation or

---

[7] Existential Depression, Facebook Page, https://www.facebook.com/pg/Existential-Depression-229835853787959/about/?entry_point=about_section_header&ref=page_internal

human race? Breed because sex with a condom is less pleasant? Breed because contraception is inconvenient? Breed because abortion is inconvenient? Breed for no reason at all? How selfish could it be breeding for such frivolous reasons or no reason at all?

As the partial destruction of the brain is a partial destruction of self, complete destruction of the brain is a complete destruction of self.[8] Death in neuroscience means reversal to nonexistence before birth; procreation is a reversible process by death. But philosophically, procreation before birth is nonexistence of no one, i.e. no one is actually subject to nonexistence; whereas nonexistence after death is nonexistence of somebody theretofore existed, i.e. one specific person is subject to nonexistence, annihilated, destroyed and become no more.[9]

There are documented cases of procreation to harvest organ, for example, bone mallow or a kidney to provide for one's child with a disease, for example, leukaemia or renal failure.[10] But if we think procreation to exploit to save another life is evil, we must conclude that

---

[8] Carrier, Richard. Sense and Goodness Without God: A Defense of Metaphysical Naturalism, AuthorHouse, 2005, p. 152

[9] Benatar, David. "Why it is better never to come into existence." American Philosophical Quarterly 34.3 (1997): p. 350.

[10] The New York Times, More Babies Being Born to Be Donors of Tissue, 4 Jun 1991, http://www.nytimes.com/1991/06/04/health/more-babies-being-born-to-be-donors-of-tissue.html

procreation to exploit for frivolous reasons or for no reason at all is eviler. Nobody can procreate for sake of nonexistent person. Unless it's for sake of a person brought into existence[11], it's exploitation of a person brought into existence for sake of somebody else; instrumentalisation thereof. A potential person who wasn't born will never die. Eternal life is impossible, but immortality is possible by not coming into existence. Of course, we are already born, it's too late. But we can prevent our potential descendants condemned to the life and thereby condemned to death. Indeed, procreation is the root of all evil. If there's no procreation, there would be no death, war, massacre, cancer, malaria, AIDS/HIV, refugee crisis, female genital mutilation, rape, and in numerous human rights violations. If there's no procreation, Hitler, Stalin, Mao would never be brought into existence, no person to die under regimes thereof. But as 6 million Jews were killed by the holocaust, procreation and governmental aid and abet of such crime killing 6 million people in 40 days. Although our death ageism obscuring facing this fact, we should face the truth. We have a duty not to bring a potential person who will suffer into existence. But we don't have any duty to bring a potential person who will

---

[11] Benatar, David, Better Never to Have Been, Oxford University Press, 2006, pp. 129-130

Do your friends' (potential) children a favour, and a duty, by convincing them not to commit a sin of procreation, saving them from life, the only way you can save them from all sufferings and death of your children. The cosmos is a gigantic annihilation camp. Let us end the vicious cycle of life; the curse of the selfish gene.

Dear sisters and brothers, let us take the honourable course of therapeutic extinction.[14]

Anti-natalists of all countries, unite![15]

---

[14] Influenced by Pizzolatto, Nic, True Detective, Season 1, Episode 1, Rust Cohle's voice

[15] Obviously inspired by Marx, Karl, The Communist Manifesto. Here I shall note that I generally hold libertarian or classical liberal view in governance of existent human animals. Of course, I have completely contrarian views from majority libertarian views on the views pertaining to moral status of non-human and/or pre-sentient sentient beings

Selected quotes

If destruction is violence, creation, too, is violence. Procreation, therefore, involves violence. The creation of what is bound to perish certainly involves violence. -Mahatma Gandhi

Suppose for a moment that all procreation stops, it will only mean that all destruction will cease. Moksha is nothing but release from the cycle of births and deaths. This alone is believed to be the highest bliss, and rightly. -Mahatma Gandhi

Sleep is good, death is better; but of course, the best would be never to have been born at all. -Heinrich Heine

Every cradle is a grave. -Sarah Perry

The fact of having been born is a very bad augury for immortality. -George Santayana

It is curious that while good people go to great lengths to spare their children from suffering, few of them seem to notice that the one (and only)

guaranteed way to prevent all the suffering of their children is not to bring those children into existence in the first place. -David Benatar

We are born between faeces and urine. -St Augustine

We may ask ourselves whether we have a moral right to create people and thus condemn them to life and death without their consent. -Martin Neuffer

Murder maybe a crime, but procreation is a sin. -Existential Depression, Facebook Page

Life is a prison of consciousness and sentience, a life sentence followed by the death penalty -Ibid.

You cannot save a life, only save someone from life. -Ibid.

[H]aving children was a thing worse than murder. Murder is the curtailing of a life that would have ended anyway; having a child creates a death that would never have been. -Quentin S Crisp

Table of contents

The Anti-natalist Manifesto

Selected quotes

Table of contents

Chapter 1. Arguments for anti-natalism

Argument 1. Death

The badness of death

Ontological symmetry and axiological asymmetry of pre-vital and post-mortem nonexistence

Death ageism

Procreation as a cause of death

Comparison of procreative and non-procreative infliction of death with annihilation account on the badness of death

Comparison of procreative and non-procreative infliction of death with deprivation account on the badness of death

Voluntary and involuntary cessation of existence

Procreation as a violation of right to life

Suicide argument

Lethal and non-lethal sex thought experiment

Death and procreation as an infinite harm

On the claim "Death and suffering gives life meaning"

Argument 2. Suffering

Cancer and Torture

Menstrual pain and parental corporal punishment

Everyday pains and sufferings

Sufferings of infants and children

Compulsory education

Existential angst

Lack of free will

Disutility of labour

Desire frustration

Self-control frustration and regret

Retrospective regret on decisions one has made

Pregnancy anxiety

Freedom frustration

Children's disenfranchised status

Immigration frustration

Damnation risk: possibility of eternal torment

Human factory farming risk (anthropophagic risk)

Suffering footprint of procreation

Argument 3. Benatar's asymmetry

The Basic Asymmetry

Benatar's Four Other Asymmetries

Augmented asymmetry: why procreation is always a harm even if there's no suffering

The objection that hypothetically infinite pleasure is impossible

Negative Utilitarianism

Argument 4. Consent

Lack of consent of the child

Unsolicitedness of life (life as an unsolicited gift)

Right to cognitive self-determination (cognitive liberty)

Right to ontological self-determination (ontological liberty)

Retrospective Consent

Argument 5. Treating a child as an instrument

Procreation as an instrumentalisation of the child

Instrumentalisation as violation of human dignity

Argument 6. Orphans

Argument 7. Overpopulation and environment

Argument 8. Animal holocaust

Argument 9. (Un)aesthetic

Chapter 2. Anti-natalist activism

Contraception

Alternative entertainment methods

Non-human animal companion animal/robot

Girls' education, prosperity

Prosperity and education in general

Vegans/Animal Rights activists

Kantians and deontologists

Child rights activists

Existing anti-natalist movements

Chapter 3. Anti-natalist policy

Universal Declaration of Human Rights

Rome Statute of the International Criminal Court

Natural-born-citizen clause of the US Constitution

Impunity and immunity for procreative infliction of death and other harms

Procreation as a tort (wrongful life cause of action)

Procreation tax

Procreation tax usage for universal basic income

Procreation tax usage for universal cryonics

Children's rights

State discouragement of procreation

Chapter 4. Moral complexities

Is it immoral to save a life?: the negative externality of beneficence

Prima facie duties

Procreative externality of saving life

Carnistic externality of saving life

Carnistic externality of poverty alleviation

Philanthropic exploitation of non-human animals

Unavoidable harms to non-human animals by even vegans

Moral Dilemmas in Anti-natalism Advocacy

Maleficence on the sentient being for the beneficence of the same sentient being

Maleficence on the sentient being for the beneficence of the other sentient beings

Impossibility of universal beneficence

Professional duty and non-professional duty

Chapter 5. Miscellaneous

Pro-death view on abortion

Non-human animal breeding

Legal personhood of non-human sentient beings

Legal personhood of pre-sentient sentient beings

Possible dysgenic impact of anti-natalism

A response to techno-optimists

Asymmetry in our capacity to reduce and inflict suffering

Chapter 1. Arguments for anti-natalism

Argument 1. Death

The badness of death

"No one wants to die."[16] Those who wishes death do so because the quality of that person's life is so unbearable. Those who request for euthanasia or assisted suicide do so because life becomes worse than death (under their preference)

Ontological symmetry and axiological asymmetry of pre-vital and post-mortem nonexistence[17]

View	Pre-vital nonexistence	Post-mortem nonexistence
Objective	Nonexistence	Nonexistence
Epicurean	Subjectively neither existence nor nonexistence	Subjectively neither existence nor nonexistence
Benatarian	Nonexistence of nobody who exists	Nonexistence of somebody used to exist

Of course, there're arguments claiming that nonexistence before birth (more accurately, pre-sentience nonexistence or pre-vital nonexistence) is

---

[16] Jobs, Steve, Steve Jobs' 2005 Stanford Commencement Address, Stanford University, https://www.youtube.com/watch?v=UF8uR6Z6KLc

[17] The term was coined by Kauffman, Ferederik, see "Pre-vital and post-mortem nonexistence", American Philosophical Quarterly

the same as nonexistence after death (more accurately, post-annihilation nonexistence or post-mortem nonexistence). Of course, pre-vital and post-mortem nonexistence are (ontologically, neurologically and cognitively) symmetrical.

But it does not follow that pre-vital and post-mortem nonexistence are axiologically symmetrical. That is to say, there're crucial asymmetries in ethical implications (axiological asymmetry) of pre-vital and post-mortem nonexistence. Prof Benatar argued, "whereas pre-vital nonexistence is that do not actually happen to anybody, death is something that happens to somebody."[18]

Also, a theory on why death is a bad thing, which is called deprivation account on the badness of death, suggests that death is bad because death deprives good things in life dead person would otherwise enjoy. David Benatar supplemented deprivation account with annihilation account on the badness of death. Prof Benatar argued, "annihilation of an individual is a distinct bad". He further argued that the badness of death "is not entirely reducible to deprivation." It should be noted that death is

---

[18] Benatar, David. "Why it is better never to come into existence." American Philosophical Quarterly 34.3 (1997)

most often considered a bad thing even if an individual has no prospect of further enjoy good things in life. Death can be a bad thing even if there're no more good things in life to be deprived by death.[19]

Death ageism

We tend to regret the death of a child or young person hugely, while regret death of an old person (say, at age 90) far less than earlier death, or do not regret at all. But saying some death is less bad than other deaths, that may mean some life have less value than other lives. David Benatar said, we tend to consider death at 40 tragic, while a death at 90 is taken casual, and he said that's because of relative comparison. And Prof Benatar said, people wouldn't think death at 40 tragic in the past. And he said the reason we tend to think short life in poor countries tragic is we are comparing life expectancy to life expectancy we're accustomed to. Similarly, Prof Benatar argued, death at age 90 would be taken tragic if average life expectancy is 120.[20] And the life expectancy of 90 years is

---

[19] Benatar, David, Deprived and Annihilated, http://philosophyofdeath.org/2016-conference-abstracts/ (Conference Abstract for International Association for the Philosophy of Death and Dying 2016 Conference)

[20] Benatar, David. "Why it is better never to come into existence." American Philosophical Quarterly 34.3 (1997)

much closer to 1 than 1,000 years.[21] Prof Benatar argued, all other things being equal, death is a serious harm, and "there's an intrinsic tragedy in every death."[22]

Marcus Aurelius said, "The longest-lived and the shortest-lived man, when they come to die, lose one and the same thing.". Although there may be (relatively) worse and less worse way of death, the fundamental quality of death as an annihilation (complete and irreparable destruction) of sentience is the same across all sentient beings, regardless of self-awareness, age and/or species.

Every sentient being is individual and final.[23] Because all sentient beings are individual and final, all sentient beings are persons. What I mean by that every sentient being is individual is, that the subjective phenomenal experience of individual sentient being cannot be felt by another (aside indirect influences of one's phenomenal experience toward another). That

---

[21] Benatar, David, Wasserman, David, Debating Procreation, Oxford University Press, 2015, p. 52

[22] Benatar, David. "Why it is better never to come into existence." American Philosophical Quarterly 34.3 (1997)

[23] Gray, John N., The Silence of Animals: On Progress and Other Modern Myths, Penguin, 2013, "Humanity is a fiction composed from billions of individuals for each of whom life is singular and final."

individuality of sentient beings also applies to sentient beings' annihilation. And what I mean by that every sentient being is final is, that the annihilation of individual sentient being is final.

Procreation as a cause of death

Disclaimer: This table is based on only human animals	Procreative Infliction of Death	Non-procreative Infliction of Death
Name	Procreation Natural death Death by natural causes Death by disease	Murder, Manslaughter, Homicide, Death Penalty, Capital Punishment, Execution, The Holocaust, Genocide, Massacre
Time of Death	World average: 70 years after procreation 1st Word: 80 years Max: 125 years	Usually immediately; Year and a day rule Three years and a day rule
Manner of death	Usually 'non-violent' Cancer Disease Ageing	Usually violent Shooting Stabbing Lethal injection
Punishment	Impunity	Death Life imprisonment Imprisonment for long term sometimes impunity

Disclaimer: This table is based on only human animals	Procreative Infliction of Death	Non-procreative Infliction of Death
Harm caused	Inflicted Death on a potential person who didn't have to die (Inflicted immense amount of gratuitous suffering)	Curtailed decades of life Made death happen earlier (Deprived future pleasure) (also Prevented future suffering)
Fatalities per year	56-58 million	500,000

6 million Jews were killed by the holocaust. 6 million people are killed by procreation every 40 days. Procreation is indeed the cause of 100% of deaths in the world. Procreation is a violence causing more death than any kind of cause of death, including cancer, war, malaria, AIDS/HIV.

Procreation is morally problematic because it causes death. (more accurately put, annihilation) Every procreation causes death. Because every procreation causes death, procreation can be considered as a form of infliction of death. Non-procreative inflictions of death are called 'murder', 'manslaughter' or 'homicide'. For sake of objectiveness, I would use the term I coined 'procreative infliction of death' henceforth. But it does not follow that procreation is any less harmful practice than homicide. Procreation is enough to be called murder, homicide or filicide.

One distinguished difference of procreation (effectively also procreative infliction of death) and homicide (non-procreative infliction of death) is that the former is widely praised, whereas the latter is widely condemned. One of naive pro-natalist assumption is because death is a bad thing, procreation, which can be considered as an antonym of death, is a good thing. But the crucial defect of that naive assumption is that it is ignoring the obvious fact that procreation is an essential prerequisite (and the ultimate cause) of death.

I shall compare procreative infliction of death and non-procreative infliction of death on annihilation and deprivation account of the badness of death.

Account	Procreative infliction of death	Non-procreative infliction of death
Annihilation	Create a new and gratuitous annihilation	Not creating new annihilation, only making annihilation happen sooner
Deprivation	Deprive infinite time after death	Deprive only time between the time of non-procreative infliction of death and the time the person would otherwise die

Account	Procreative infliction of death	Non-procreative infliction of death
Pleasure	Make the person enjoy the pleasure, but nonetheless it is not a benefit because pre-vital nonexistent person is not deprived of pleasure	Deprive prospects of pleasure in the future the person otherwise would enjoy
Suffering	Inflict new and gratuitous suffering	Aside suffering during the non-procreative infliction of death, suffering of the person's family and friends, make the person no longer suffer that person otherwise would suffer

Comparison of procreative and non-procreative infliction of death with annihilation account on the badness of death

"Murder is the curtailing of a life that would have ended anyway; having a child creates a death that would never have been." -Quentin S Crisp[24]

Non-procreative infliction of death (usually called murder) annihilates the victim. But the victim would be invariably annihilated in due course. In this case, although the time of annihilation was changed by non-procreative infliction of death, the very fact the annihilation would happen sooner or later wasn't.

---

[24] Crisp, Quentin S, living in the future, Issue 2, Anti-natalISM: A THOUGHT EXPERIMENT, http://www.litfmag.net/issue-2/antinatalism-a-thought-experiment/

Procreation creates the very liability to the annihilation. Every (human) procreation cause an annihilation after just a few decades, "well within 130 years". Such annihilation is never possible without procreation. Procreative infliction of death changes the very fact whether a potential person would annihilate or not.

That is to say, *ceteris paribus,* whereas murder reduces the momentary number of (alive) life in the world, and increase the momentary number of death in particular duration (e.g. a particular calendar year), murder itself do not increase the inter-temporal number of total death. Since all life brought into existence invariably die.

Contrary to the impact of the murder in inter-temporal number of total death, *ceteris paribus,* whereas procreation increase the momentary number of (alive) life in the world, procreation do increase the inter-temporal number of total death, even though the majority of

Therefore, procreative infliction of death is more harmful than the non-procreative infliction of death under assessment with the annihilation account on the badness of death.

Comparison of procreative and non-procreative infliction of death with deprivation account on the badness of death

Non-procreative infliction of death (usually called murder) deprives the victim the good things in life the victim would otherwise enjoy. For example, if the victim is 20 years old when he was killed and otherwise he would live until the age of 80, non-procreative infliction of death deprive him (the good things of) 60 years of life.

Whereas procreation makes the resultant person enjoy good things in life, the absence of good things in life because of non-procreation is not a deprivation because there's nobody thereby deprived. Whereas pre-sentience nonexistence does not deprive anyone, post-annihilation nonexistence deprives one specific person theretofore existent the good things of life. In this case, the deceased was deprived of not just (the good things of) the (duration of) life from the age she died at the age of her maximum possible span of life. The deceased was deprived of (the good things of) the life of infinite (hypothetical) time after the time of her annihilation.

Of course, there can be an argument that "life is a gift". The problem with that argument is that the 'recipient' of the 'gift' of life do not have any interest coming into existence. Even if a gift never harmed the recipient, if that gift was unsolicited, there's no responsibility arise from the receipt of that unsolicited gift. But if a 'gift' is potentially harmful, (for example, a 'gift' was a food that was contaminated with fatal amount of toxin, but it was not stated), the sender is morally and legally liable for murder, or attempted murder even if the 'gift' haven't caused death.

Voluntary and involuntary cessation of existence

Consent type	Birth (Procreation)	Death
Consented	Voluntary procreation (impossible)	Voluntary euthanasia, assisted suicide, suicide
Non-consensual and unable to give consent	Non-voluntary procreation	Non-voluntary euthanasia
Non-consensual and able to give consent	Involuntary procreation (impossible)	Involuntary euthanasia, murder/maslaughter/ homicide, also all cases of non-voluntary death (such as cancer, death by natural causes)

There are two kinds of cessation of existence (annihilation/death). One is the voluntary cessation of existence, and another is the involuntary cessation of existence. Voluntary cessation of existence, obviously, includes suicide, assisted suicide and voluntary euthanasia. However, involuntary cessation of existence not just includes murder/manslaughter/ homicide but also all involuntary death. That is to say, that all so-called natural death is a form of involuntary death. And all involuntary death is ultimately caused and inflicted by one's progenitors. It should be noted, however, that even the psychological tendency and circumstances to cause voluntary death is also procreatively inflicted. Because there would be no death without procreation, all death is a parentally inflicted death. 100% of death in the world is caused by procreatively-caused causes.

Procreation as a violation of right to life

Article 2 – Right to life, Charter of Fundamental Rights of the European Union

1. Everyone has the right to life.
2. No one shall be condemned to the death penalty, or executed.

Finally, procreation can be interpreted as a violation of the right to life. As every procreation leads to death, procreation is not just as severe as, or even more severe than capital punishment (capital punishment only makes death happen a few decades earlier, whereas procreation condemns a potential person who needs not die at all to death), and as all EU jurisdictions prohibit capital punishment for the reason of human dignity, there is no intrinsic reason to think procreation is not a violation of human right, whereas death penalty is. Procreation is essentially violation of Article 2 (right to life, prohibition of death penalty) of the Charter of Fundamental Rights of the European Union; although possibility of EU jurisdictions and/or European Court of Human Rights admit such claim seems to be highly unlikely (more likely to be described as a frivolous claim/litigation). I can't find any good reason the right to life shouldn't include freedom from procreative deprivation of life. (even though procreation also confers/inflicts such life)

Suicide argument

Prof Benatar argued, although there's no cost not having been born, ceasing to exist have costs.[25] Of course, annihilation and deprivation make death a serious harm, but also suicide causes severe trauma toward family and friends.[26]

Sarah Perry argued, that free disposal of life suggested by Bryan Caplan is *de facto* impossible because suicide has very high cost, for example, the most certain and pain-free methods of suicide, say, lethal liquid is very hard to access. And while suicide is not a crime, aiding suicide is a crime. And in the case of failure of the suicide, it can cause injuries and

---

[25] Benatar, David, We Are Creatures That Should Not Exist, The Critique, http://www.thecritique.com/articles/we-are-creatures-that-should-not-exist-the-theory-of-anti-natalism/

[26] Benatar, David, Better Never to Have Been, p. 220

disabilities, and make the person who attempted suicide involuntarily confined to a mental hospital.[27]

By coming into (sentient) existence, a sentient being develops an interest to continue its existence.[28] Axiological asymmetry of the pre-vital and post-mortem nonexistence shows us that the cost of ceasing to exist (whether voluntary or involuntary) include annihilation of the person and deprivation of prospects of life.

Libertarian pro-natalist may argue that the child can commit suicide if it is unhappy it was brought into existence. It is an appalling argument in a lot of ways. First, there are crucial axiological asymmetries of pre-vital and post-mortem nonexistence. Second, it implicitly assumes 'free will'. Because it is impossible to have a metaphysical free will, a person's decision whether or not to take its own life is determined by factors hugely influenced by one's parents, i.e., nature (genes inherited from its progenitors) and nurture (including, parental attitude toward suicide). Third, it takes quite a long time for a child to 'mature' enough to take its

---

[27] Perry, Sarah, Every Cradle is a Grave, Nine Banded Books, 2014

[28] Benatar, David, Better Never to Have Been

own life. Fourth, the decision on continuation/cessation of life is hugely distorted by adaptive preference.

Lethal and non-lethal sex thought experiment

Suppose human animals of each sex have two (i.e. a pair) genitalia each. Although sex with either genitalia is equally pleasurable, there would be no particular sexual orientation on particular genitalia to use, and they are easily distinguishable with each other. And suppose one genitalia (say, non-lethal genitalia) would create an immortal human animal, while another (say, lethal genitalia) would create a mortal human animal, which would die in just a few decades. If we really have such choice whether to create mortal or immortal offspring, it would be thought completely unacceptable to have sex with lethal genitalia. Sex with lethal genitalia may become a crime or even a murder.

Here I shall argue, that non-lethal sexual intercourse is a course of action which we all could follow. Although the overwhelming majority of human animals are heterosexual, and heterosexual couple mostly prefer penile-vaginal intercourse, there're various ways of heterosexual intercourse other than penile-vaginal intercourse. (it should be noted pregnancy with penile-anal intercourse is possible if the female party of the intercourse has untreated rectocele) Also, although not perfect, vasectomy prevent the possibility of penile-vaginal intercourse resulting in lethal pregnancy with 99.85-99.9% of probability.[29] Of course, it would be needless to say that homosexual intercourse are non-lethal or abstinence is non-lethal.

Although the non-lethal sex is only possible with the 'cost' of non-procreation, at least in this pre-singularity era, that 'cost' is never a cost for the non-existent potential person, but the cost of hopeful parents and the community.

Death and procreation as an infinite harm

If we would (or should) think (sentient) life have an infinite value, we would (and should) think the loss of life as an infinite harm. Because a potential sentient being does not have any interest to have a life, no benefit is conferred upon birth (more accurately, the initiation of sentience). Quite contrary, an infinite harm is caused upon procreation, as all procreation invariably cause death.

On the claim "Death and suffering gives life meaning"

---

[29] http://www.contraceptivetechnology.org/wp-content/uploads/2013/09/CTFailureTable.pdf

There are purported claims that harms of life, such as death or suffering, gives life purported good things in life, such as meaning, mental or 'spiritual' growth, etc.. Steve Jobs famously claimed that death gives purported benefits in life.[30] The first problem of such claims is that pre-vital nonexistent people do not need any such purported good things in life, and are not benefited by coming into existence and enjoying such purported good things in life. The second problem of such claims is that it is dubious we need harms such as death or suffering in order to enjoy good things in life, and if that is true, our life is worse because we can't enjoy pure benefits without harms.

In axiology of harms such as birth (initiation of the sentience), death (annihilation of the sentience), suffering (including both physical pain and mental suffering) and other bad things in life, it should be noted that the intrinsic value of harms and the instrumental value of harms should be separated. The intrinsic value of harms, by definition, always bad. Contrary, there may be some instrumental value in harms. For example, death (annihilation) prevents future suffering that person would otherwise suffer. But it does not follow we can kill (painlessly while sleeping)

---

[30] Jobs, Steve, Steve Jobs' 2005 Stanford Commencement Address, Stanford University, https://www.youtube.com/watch?v=UF8uR6Z6KLc

somebody under agonising suffering without her consent. It is prohibited to (non-procreatively) inflict severe suffering on another without consent, even if it may give 'meaning' to the victim and make the victim grow 'spiritually'. I shall argue we should go just one step further to think procreative infliction of harm is as morally indecent as non-procreative infliction of harm.

Argument 2. Suffering

Disclaimer: This table is based on only human animals	Procreative Infliction of Suffering	Non-procreative Infliction of Suffering
Name	Procreation Pain, Suffering, Depression, Stress, Frustration, Cancer	Torture Battery, Hitting, Abuse, Rape, Violence, Imprisonment, Torture
Time of Suffering	Immediately after fetus become sentient Until death	Immediate but usually short-lasting
Manner of suffering	Usually 'non-violent' Cancer Disease Ageing	Usually violent Torture Assault Sexual Assault
Punishment	Impunity	Death Life imprisonment Imprisonment sometimes Impunity
Harm caused	Inflicted decades of immense amount of gratuitous pain and suffering	Usually short-lasting pain and/or suffering

Every procreation causes suffering, not negligible, but an immense amount. Here, I shall compare procreative infliction of suffering and non-procreative infliction of suffering. As Prof Benatar argued, there's no intrinsic reason to treat procreatively inflicted harm any differently with comparable non-procreatively inflicted harm[31]. Of course, unlike death, suffering is probabilistic, but, as Prof Benatar puts, it is absolutely guaranteed a person would suffer immense amount in one way or another[32]. Some form of pains, for example, menstrual pains, are expected, considered completely normal and even as a healthy thing.

Cancer and Torture

A potential person who never brought into existence will never suffer cancer; whereas "40% of men and 37% of women in Britain develop cancer at some point."[33].

Torture is prohibited under the Rome Statute as a crime against humanity or war crime.

---

[31] Benatar, David, Better Never to Have Been, p. 112

[32] Benatar, David, Direko, Redi, Why your life is worse than you think, Talk Radio 702, Feb 26, 2009

[33] Benatar, David, The Critique, 'We Are Creatures That Should Not Exist', 15 Jul 2015

Is there a good reason to permit procreative infliction of the substantial (nearly-half) risk of a torturous pain of malignant neoplasms, while strictly prohibiting non-procreative infliction of torturous pain?

Menstrual pain and parental corporal punishment

Menstruation is procreatively caused and expected to occur to newly procreated baby girls in due course, about a decade after procreation; and usually entail very often significant pain and discomfort lowering quality of life of the substantial portion of girls' and women's lifetime. In the sizeable minority of jurisdictions (predominantly in Europe and South America), parental corporal punishment is prohibited, penalties include imprisonment and termination of parental rights. If parental corporal punishment should be prohibited, is there a good reason to allow procreative infliction of menstrual pain of which degree of pain may be comparable to usual parental corporal punishment?

Everyday pains and sufferings

Prof Benatar mentioned a list of everyday discomforts, "hunger, thirst, bowel and bladder distension (as these organs become filled), tiredness, stress, thermal discomfort (that is, feeling either too hot or too cold), and itch.". According to one study, average Briton suffers 10,787 ailments in the course of their life.[34]

Sufferings of infants and children

During parturition, particularly in cases of vaginal birth, fetus suffer a severe amount of stresses. Neonates -even though this is just start of an immense amount of suffering- start a life of decades of suffering by being slapped to induce self-breathing. Millions of neonate boys start life by suffering a violation of bodily integrity by being genitally mutilated (so-called neonate circumcision) for dubious medical benefits, often without any anaesthetics. Millions of girls are subjected to genital mutilation for no medical reason at all.

Sharp injection needle causes an immense amount of fear for millions of adults, and for virtually every child, the injection needle is a source of an immense amount of fear and pain.

Because infants cannot express unpleasantness without crying, express unpleasantness and pain by crying. Average infants cry times a day. Sufferings of infants include hunger, thirst and thermal discomfort.

---

[34] http://www.mirror.co.uk/lifestyle/health/life-10787-sore-points---2093834

Particularly for thermal discomfort, a lot of parents abandon children in the hot car and very often overdress infant. Many parents make infants sleep in the separate bed (and deprived the interest for attachment to parents). In the past, children were breastfed until 7 years old. Now, millions of children are not breastfed at all, and most children are breastfed for only a few months. A lot of children are raised by foster parents, grandparents and day care centres merely for parental convenience.

Millions of parents who smoke know very well that (even if one smokes where there's no child) smoking is very harmful to one's child, and nonetheless smoke without much guilt. Smoking parents often even smoke in front of the child, sometimes ignoring explicit dislike of one's offspring.

About 30% children has been reported to wish they had never been born according to a research.[35]

Compulsory education

---

[35] Cavan, Ruth Shonle. "The wish never to have been born." American journal of sociology (1932): 547-559.

We can't deny that acquisition of basic knowledge is instrumental in the healthy development of the child. But only a few people notice that compulsory education was invented by arguably the first totalitarian in human history, Plato. And Plato's the most (in)famous disciple, Marx is also one of the earliest advocates of compulsory education. It is clear one of the major side effect (or even intentional hidden curriculum) is indoctrination and obedience conditioning.

The best example of the miserable failure of compulsory education (although compulsory education is not the only factor to blame) is that only small minority of people notice immorality of animal slavery and procreation, and act on it. The slave status of non-human sentient beings and the non-consensual creation of the sentient beings are the most prevalent forms of human evil. Vegetarianism or veganism is rarely taught in school, and it is inconceivable compulsory education institutions to teach anti-natalism.

One of the most severe forms of suffering compulsory education inflicts is intentional circadian rhythm disruption. According to one research, 10am or later is the ideal school starting time.[36] "[A] 07:00 alarm call for older adolescents is the equivalent of a 04:30 start for a teacher in their 50s. Failure to adjust education timetables to this biological change leads to systematic, chronic and unrecoverable sleep loss. This level of sleep loss causes impairment to physiological, metabolic and psychological health in adolescents while they are undergoing other major physical and neurological changes".[37] Almost all schools in the world start much earlier than 10 o'clock, around 7:30 to 8:30. Current school schedule was designed not for the sake of the healthy development of the children, but parental convenience.

Compulsory education most often does not provide adequate tuition of lingua franca (namely, the English language) if the jurisdiction does not use English neither as a native language nor as a second language. Compulsory education most likely does not or very limitedly provide knowledge about personal finances, computer programming, etc..

---

[36] Kelley, Paul, et al. "Synchronizing education to adolescent biology:'let teens sleep, start school later'." Learning, Media and Technology 40.2 (2015): 210-226.
APA

[37] Ibid.

The choice of the subjects taught to students are very limited. Universal Declaration of Human Rights stipulates the only parental right to choose the education of their offsprings. Many schools are religious schools to indoctrinate parental or state religion.

Compulsory education, aside from its necessity, is obviously a form of involuntary servitude. One of the hidden curricula of school is standardisation of students. Public schools in many countries, and most private schools require uniform-wearing. Even hairstyles of students regulated in some schools in some countries. But even if students are allowed a 'privilege' to wear whatever clothes, non-consensual instruction of standardised curricula and a standardised assessment on a standardised test makes students feel oneself as a standardised human, instead of a unique and singular individual with inviolable dignity.

Perhaps the biggest 'achievement' of the inculcation of compulsory education is the development of 'adaptive preference' to retrospectively consent and appreciate the compulsory education they have been subjected to. And thereby causing people to voluntarily relinquish the custody of their offspring to the pseudo-parental (*in loco parentis*) institution.

Existential angst

The cause of the existence of the cosmos is unknown, and impossible to be known by logic since even if the prime cause should be known, the cause of the prime cause is unknown. Not just our existence is unsolicited, by logic, existence cannot solicit existence of itself. That is to say, although it is plausible there can be a prime mover, an anthropomorphic 'god', superintelligence or other agent which might created this universe, even their existence is unsolicited and nonconsensual. Even purported god can't know how and why it was brought into existence. (The ultimate cause of its existence) Moreover, as an anti-natalist myself, the very fact that the purported god is a pro-natalist is a very good evidence of moral indecency (at least, non-omnibenevolence) of the purported god. The purported god engaged in morally indecent behavior of unsolicitedly (pro)creating more than quadrillions of us sentient beings without our consent and permission.

The prospect of death, whether the person is religious or not, is very frightening. For non-religious people, the prospect of annihilation is very disgusting and demoralising. For religious people, the prospect of judgment, possibility to be sent to hell is very frightening.

There's a thought experiment called Roko's Basilisk[38], that AI may punish people who didn't help bring it into existence by torturing eternally. Although some people may prefer hell than annihilation, the prospect of eternal torment is indeed very distressing.

If a person eventually realises that her parents arbitrarily procreated her for selfish reasons, with knowledge of human miseries she will about to face, that itself can cause huge emotional distress.

Lack of free will

A lot of neuroscientists agree that there's no free will. Evidence include Libet experiment, which found out that EEG could predict the button a person about to push hundreds of milliseconds before his consciousness inclined to push one of two buttons.

Lack of free will means nothing can be ultimately chosen by himself, that everything is decided by one's parents (genes and environment), and other environments. It can be disgusting.

---

[38] Roko's Basilisk, LessWrong Wiki, https://wiki.lesswrong.com/wiki/Roko%27s_basilisk

Facing one's fate is predetermined, even if there're some chances of difference because of quantum effects, the fact there's nothing one can ultimately do to improve one's condition and fate is really demoralising and disturbing. (This is not to deny one can improve condition of oneself by effort, the lack of free will means that the action one will take is determined)

Disutility of labour

After the tunnel of 12 to 20 years of education, most people suffer immense amount in the work which they accepted only to pay bills. About 70% Americans are reported to hate their job[39]. Ludwig von Mises mentioned about disutility of labour[40]. According to research, the reason most people work is merely to make money. Of course, most labour in the world right now is voluntarily accepted and performed, but the urgent need to support oneself that everybody has, is a gratuitous need that has been caused with (non-consensual) procreation. Of course, it should be noted that many young people in the world do not have a chance for the

---

[39] 70% Of Your Employees Hate Their Job, Forbes, Nov 11, 2011, http://www.forbes.com/sites/carminegallo/2011/11/11/your-emotionally-disconnected-employees/#6737fea6e89b

[40] Mises, Ludwig von, Human Action, 1949

first (gainful and stable) employment, and a lot of people are fired and suffer severe financial insecurity.

Desire frustration

The most important frustration of desire is a frustration of anti-mortal preferences. Particularly, non-religious people (more accurately put, those who hold annihilationist view on death) may feel extreme existential distress or depression contemplating on mortality of themselves and fellow sentient beings. Religious people may feel extreme fear on the possibility of the damnation of themselves or family and friends.

Many cases, the human romantic attraction is unrequited. Human friendship and romantic relationship are fragile. Many males find themselves unable to find a partner, as a result of demographic disparity, naturally caused or as a result of female foeticide or infanticide. Also, even the richest people find their money not enough (if the desire to spend money includes a desire to donate). The overwhelming majority of people in the world die before travelling 100 countries out of about 200 countries in the world. Those with the resources to travel the world often find themselves too busy to take vacations. Millions of pro-natalist couples are infertile and desperately seek costly fertility treatments such as in-vitro fertilisation (IVF).

Drugs that can enhance cognitive performance or alters cognitive state are mostly prohibited or strictly restricted. These types of drugs include LSD, Adderal, Marijuana. (Violation/restriction of cognitive liberty or right to cognitive self-determination)

The excellent example of cognitive liberty or right to cognitive self-determination is, of course, procreation. Procreation not just violates the right to cognitive self-determination but also the right to ontological self-determination (ontological liberty). The desire for pre-vital (not post-mortem) nonexistence can never be fulfilled and frustrates desires of all anti-natalists.

Height, facial attractiveness, assigned gender, intelligence, skin colour, race, native language, year of birth, whether or not one have been born, place of birth (hometown) and country of (natural born) citizenship are either impossible to change or extremely difficult to change. And dissatisfaction on these (nearly or completely) irreparably assigned features of a sentient agent is a source of severe suffering.

Self-control frustration and regret

Infirmity of will is perhaps the greatest source of self-dissatisfaction. Desire frustrations are sometimes voluntary, but nonetheless painful. Unpleasantness, regret and self-blaming from self-control (or delayed gratification) frustration is the huge source of human mental suffering.

Many vegans and vegetarians crave animal products -which they decades-long-addicted to-, even everyday, but endure such craving for ethical or health reasons. Psychological costs of animal-eating recidivism not only include self-blaming but criticism from vegan and non-vegan friends and acquaintances. The overwhelming majority of vegans 'became' vegan usually in adulthood, instead of being raised vegan by vegan parents. Therefore, most vegans find themselves that they have already eaten thousands of animals. Vegans may feel an immense amount of guilt for becoming a 'late-bloomer' vegan, particularly if they compare themselves with independent child vegetarians, children in decided to become a vegetarian even though having been raised non-vegetarian. About 80% of vegetarians go back to non-vegetarian.[41]

---

[41] http://www.animalcharityevaluators.org/research/foundational-research/vegetarian-recidivism/#second

Ethical anti-natalists may want (biological) children to satisfy reproductive and/or parenting interests but desist from procreation for ethical reasons. (Utilitarian) effective altruists who agree on Singer's drowning child argument may suffer immense amount from the voluntary curtailment of consumption and/or guilt for 'spending far more than one should'.

Many recovering former alcoholics, smokers and drug addicts suffer serious withdrawal symptoms and cravings. Many people want to lose weight and fail, and even if one succeeds, it is obtained by enduring serious discomfort from dietary restriction and exercise.

Many adults and adolescents want to delay their gratification and live life more productively. But find themselves failing. Only 5% of smokers succeed in quitting smoking (by cold turkey)[42]. Many consumers of alcoholic beverages regret the consumption on the next morning. Many people make a new year's resolution but fail within a few days. Many people try not to eat or reduce consumption of junk foods but fail and regret.

---

[42] http://www.stopsmoking.news/2015-10-05-the-top-12-success-rates-of-smoking-cessation-rated-from-worst-to-best.html

Many adults and adolescents think they spend too much time on social media, television and video gaming, but fail in self-controlling. Many people think they should reduce or eliminate unnecessary spendings and save money but fail. Many adults think they should work harder and learn hard skills such as foreign language but fail. Many adolescents and college students think they should study harder but fail. Many people try to reduce sleep but fail.

Retrospective regret on decisions one has made

Many people who have been diagnosed with cancer poignantly regret that one has lived on unhealthy lifestyle. A lot of people find themselves regretting on death bed for not living the life the fullest. Even not at the death bed, most of us -if not all of us- regret that we haven't lived life so far to the fullest. Many people regret that they left emotional scars on family and friends, even for decades. A late-bloomer anti-natalist may regret that they have brought their offspring into existence. It may be one of the most terrible parental experience to know that their children wish not have been born.

Pregnancy anxiety

Heterosexual or bisexual anti-natalist may avoid heterosexual intercourse, or even a romantic relationship because of the possibility of unintended pregnancy and procreation. First, if an anti-natalist is a male, he (a potential inseminator) may worry that his partner (a potential gestator) (even if she stated that she would get an abortion if pregnant) may refuse to get an abortion if pregnant. No contraception is perfect, and even vasectomy have 0.1%-0.15% chance of failure[43]. Whereas the fact only females gestate and males do not gestate may be advantage to males, such gestational asymmetry can be huge disadvantage in a jurisdiction where abortion is legal or rarely punished, since inseminating male have no control over whether or not gestating female get an abortion. Second, an anti-natalist couple may live in a country which abortion is illegal or restricted. Third, an anti-natalist may have religious, ethical and/or sentimental objection to contraception or (pre-sentience) abortion. Pregnancy anxiety and frustration from unintended pregnancy and/or procreation is a universal human suffering, even if one is not an anti-natalist. Contraception is failing in too many cases. "Among

---

[43] http://www.contraceptivetechnology.org/wp-content/uploads/2013/09/CTFailureTable.pdf

unintended pregnancies in the United States, 60% of the women used birth control to some extent during the month pregnancy occurred."[44]

Freedom frustration

According to the Freedom House, only 89 countries are 'Free' countries, whereas 59 countries are 'Partly Free' and 50 countries are 'Not Free'. Only 40% of the world population live in the 'Free' countries, whereas 24% live in the 'Partly Free' countries and 36% live in the 'Not Free' countries. Only 47 countries were rated 1.0 in overall 'Freedom Rating' (1 = most free, 7 = least free). And only 5 countries, Finland, Iceland, Norway, San Marino, Sweden, are rated 100% in the Aggregate Score.[45]

Children's disenfranchised status

And of course, children are severely disenfranchised of freedom. Only 51 countries or territories prohibited parental hitting (so-called corporal punishment)[46]. Parents can inflict non-corporal punishment (such as grounding, i.e. parental imprisonment) on their discretion (i.e. without due

---

[44] https://en.wikipedia.org/wiki/Pregnancy

[45] Freedom in the World, Freedom House, 2016, https://freedomhouse.org/report/freedom-world-2016/table-scores

[46] https://en.wikipedia.org/wiki/Corporal_punishment#Legal_status

process of law) in any jurisdiction. Children are not allowed to choose an educational institution, subjects to learn and careers to pursue without parental consent. Children cannot work, travel, move, apply for the passport and emigrate without parental consent. Children in 'Free' countries are not much better treated than women in the countries the most oppressive to women. The notion of 'corporal punishment' or 'guardian consent' by parents can be compared to 'corporal punishment' of wives or 'guardian consent' by the husband.

Of course, this is not to deny the necessity of some restriction of freedom of children. But nonetheless, First, we are treating children far worse than we should and could. A lot of institutions such as procreation, 'corporal punishment' or school schedule (which seriously disrupts circadian rhythm of the child) is designed for

Second, situating a potential person (that do not have any interest in coming into existence) to a cognitive condition that mental maturity is limited, and thereby necessitates serious restriction of freedom, is an infliction of a serious, gratuitous and irreparable harm, and (ethically) completely inadmissible.

Immigration frustration

According to Gallup, 700 million people in the world want to emigrate to a foreign country permanently if they could.[47] Even visiting privileged countries are not easily permitted to nationals of lesser privileged countries. (Permanent or temporary) residence in the privileged countries is extremely selective. Only 5% of the people in the world have the right to abode in the United States, the country with arguably most opportunities for 'self-actualisation'. Only about 1 billion people have the right to abode in the similarly privileged countries or territories, including, the US, the UK, Canada, Australia, New Zealand, EU/EEA/Switzerland, Japan, South Korea, Singapore, Hong Kong and Taiwan.

Damnation risk: possibility of eternal torment

Scenarios	Estimated Probability (on equiprobability heuristic)	Consequence
Salvation	25%	Good
Annihilation	25%	Extremely Bad
Damnation	25%	Extremely Bad, Perhaps worse than annihilation
Non-singularity	25%	Very Bad

---

[47] 700 Million Worldwide Desire to Migrate Permanently, Gallup, 2009, http://www.gallup.com/poll/124028/700-million-worldwide-desire-migrate-permanently.aspx

Roko's Basilisk is an idea that was suggested by Roko in LessWrong.com in 2010, that an AI would be motivated to eternally torture people who have not helped to bring it into existence. The more likely possibility of eternal torment is, I think, a sadistic AI. A Reddit user TheFaggetman suggested the possibility of a sadistic AI in 2015[48], Brian Tomasik suggested a possibility of sadists take control of an AI[49].

Although the major focus on AI research is an existential risk[50], I think human extinction only bad as much as an annihilation of the people thereby annihilated is bad. Although there's no knock-down argument to prove eternal torment is worse than annihilation, as we can see on 'Better red than dead' v. 'Better dead than red' debate, if we at least think that whereas eternal torment may be infinite times worse than annihilation, annihilation may be only finite times (e.g. 10 times) worse than eternal torment, perhaps moral priority shall be given to prevention of eternal

---

[48] TheFaggetman, https://www.reddit.com/r/Futurology/comments/3l2b7o/the_hell_of_the_artificial_sadistic_intelligence/

[49] Tomasik, Brian, Foundational Research Institute, https://foundational-research.org/artificial-intelligence-and-its-implications-for-future-suffering

[50] see Bostrom, Nick. "Existential risk prevention as global priority." Global Policy 4.1 (2013): 15-31.

torment caused by AI-molecular-assembler than annihilation caused by AI.

Although I assumed all sentient beings would eventually annihilate, here I would discuss the possibility of continuation of sentience after 10^{1000} (10000000000 googol) years[51], which the heat death of the universe is expected to happen. This may be made possible by the possibility the super intelligence find out the way to cheat the heat death of the universe. But the prospect of the torture, for 10^{1000} years, may be enough to make the overwhelming majority of people to think it is better to die. Indeed, perhaps that would be the case even 100 years of the most agonising torture may be enough to make people think it is better to cease to exist.

It is interesting that several (the prevailing denominations/views of) the most prevalent religions, a kind of meme (this is a hypothesis I adopt as an atheist myself), including, namely Christianity and Islam, developed the notion of eternal torment, not annihilation as an ultimate punishment.

---

[51] https://en.wikipedia.org/wiki/Graphical_timeline_from_Big_Bang_to_Heat_Death

It may be an evidence of the prevailing preference of the people is that annihilation is a better fate than the eternal torment.

Contrary to that, generally, the death penalty is seen as the more severe punishment than life imprisonment without eligibility for parole. Of course, there're a few notable differences between death penalty-life imprisonment (without parole) and annihilation-eternal torment.

The intensity of suffering of imprisonment, although quite bad, is much better than the most agonising tortures of eternal torment. But it should be noted eternal torment is better (or worse) than life imprisonment in one way. Whereas life inmate dies after decades of suffering, eternal tormentee don't die. Eternal torment, although the momentary quality of life is very low, life expectancy is infinite, which may make strongly anti-mortal people to prefer eternal torment over annihilation. But it should be noted that considering people's attitude toward euthanasia, assisted suicide and the fact religions usually adopted eternal torment, not annihilation as an ultimate punishment, the overwhelming majority of people, or at least sizeable minority of people may prefer annihilation over eternal torment.

Here, I shall suggest the concept of 'damnation risk', to supplement Nick Bostrom's existential risk'. Dr Bostrom himself implied that there could be a worse fate than human extinction in his table. (see Fig. 1)[52]

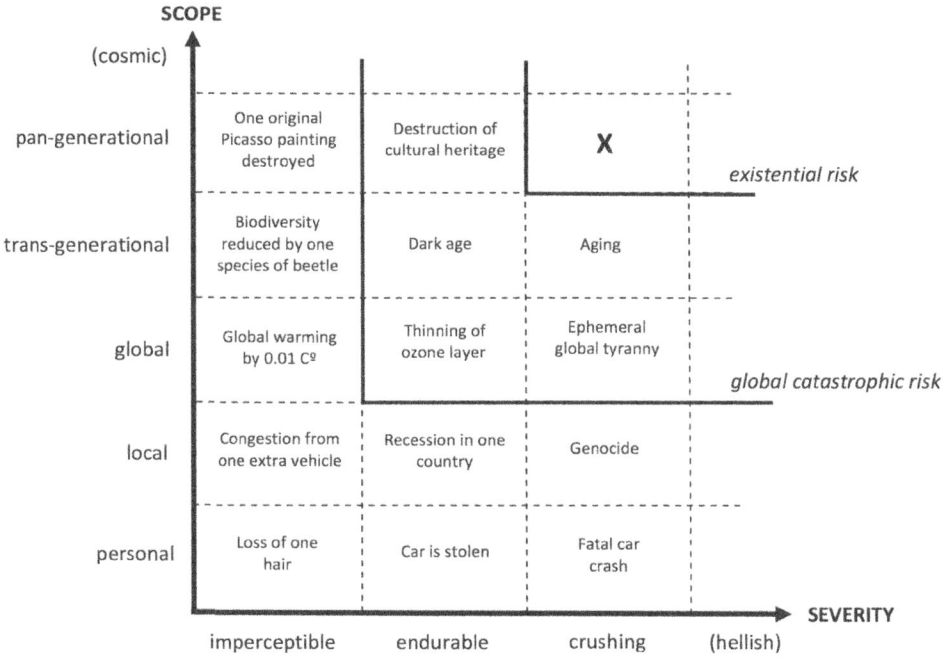

Fig. 1 (See footnote 52)

According to Dr Bostrom, hellish severity of risk (excruciating torture) is worse than crushing severity of risk (death/annihilation). And cosmic scope of risk (risk affecting all sentient beings in the cosmos) is worse

---

[52] Bostrom, Nick. "Existential risk prevention as global priority." Global Policy 4.1 (2013): 15-31.

than pan-generational scope of risk (risk affecting only human animals or, human and non-human animals in this planet).[53]

I would like to suggest that it is possible an AI or an sadist-controlled AI may torture sentient beings eternally or over very long period of time (10^{100} or 10^{1000} years), possibly all existent sentient beings. It is even possible a sadistic AI or a sadist-controlled AI may (pro)create a lot of (quadrillions to googols to infinite) sentient beings for the purpose of infliction of torture.

I shall call the risk which a sentient being is condemned to suffering that may be considered 'worse than death' by many people, a 'torment risk'. And I shall call 'torment risk' happening on the cosmic scale as a 'damnation risk'.

Of course, what amount of suffering makes people to 'prefer' annihilation over the continuation of sentience is a matter of subjective preference of (mostly lingual) sentient beings. (I'm not sure language is prerequisite of

---

[53] This interpretation is my personal view, which was not endorsed by Dr Bostrom

development of preference) I doubt there can be an objective threshold which suffering is worse than annihilation.

In most cases, sentient agent's preference on continuation/cessation of life is determined by not by the total amount of suffering it would suffer, but the intensity of the suffering of the given moment. It should be noted that most (or significant minority of) people in the most desperate situation do not choose (assisted) suicide or euthanasia. If there're people do choose continuation of sentience in any amount of pain, there's a reason to think at least some of them would choose eternal torment than annihilation (I'm one of them). If the value of (sentient) life is infinite, it is not irrational to choose (sentient) life at the cost of (infinite) pain (finite pain intensity * infinite time).

It should be noted that, possibility of eternal torment not just include possibility of eternal physical pain but also possibility of eternal mental suffering not just include the possibility of eternal physical pain but also possibility of eternal mental suffering. For example, a sadistic and disutilitarian AI may inflict a fear of public execution or the humiliation of public rape every second.

The more worrisome possibility is that AI can deliberately engineer sentient beings' cognitive capacity to feel the pain to increase the pain felt. For example, a disutilitarian AI can exponentially double cognitive capacity to feel pain every second, and inflict pain to the fullest extent sentient beings can suffer in that moment. I.e. every 10 second, the capacity and the intensity of pain can be 1024-folded and it can continue eternally. Even if the likeliness of this type of extreme sadistic disutilitarian pain-engineering is very small, it is an excellent reason not to have a child.

Although it is uncertain superintelligence would be able to overcome the heat death of the universe, if it's possible, a disutilitarian superintelligence can inflict literally eternal torment. The antonym of utilitarianism is disutilitarianism, not deontology.

Human factory farming risk (anthropophagic risk)

Also, it should be noted that because the overwhelming majority of human animals are not vegan, it is very hard to expect human animals' 'mind children'[54] to be a vegan. Because AIs would not be a member of

---

[54] Moravec, Hans, Mind Children: The Future of Robot and Human Intelligence, Harvard University Press, 1990 (Reprint edition)

the species Homo sapiens, human animals are not their conspecific, and therefore, it is not a cannibalism to eat human animals (anthropophagy). Human milk may be produced by our standard industry practices of production of cow milk. First, semens can be collected by a masturbation of human male. Second, human females can be forcefully impregnated with aforementioned semen. Third, after gestation and parturition, the neonate may be killed for 'human baby meat'. Fourth, human breast milk can be forcefully extracted by electric breast pump.

Accordingly, human 'meat' may be produced by our standard industry practices of production of 'beef'. The human male may be genitally mutilated (castrated), since testosterone make 'meat' less tasty. Human female and male may be genetically modified, and forcefully medicated with growth hormone for faster accumulation of fat. Human female and male may be slaughtered even before they reach puberty.

Although being raised 'free-range' may be better than factory farmed, the possibility of 'free-range' human animal product production is worrisome enough as well.

Suffering footprint of procreation

The suffering footprint of a procreation is about 70 years. The suffering (time) footprint of 70 years is comparable to suffering (time) footprint of 21 metric tonnes of 'beef' consumption, which is 1.19 days per kg[55]. 'Vegetarian's and vegans should be aware that time-based suffering footprint of having one child is comparable to consuming 21 metric tonnes of 'beef'. The suffering footprint is even bigger if we should include sufferings of 3rd or so on generations of descendants and animals they devour, considering the resultant child is likely to procreate and consume animal products. Also, it should be noted in the face of unprecedented uncertainty of the outcome of technological singularity, we should contemplate that there is a plausible possibility that our offspring may suffer eternal torment (beyond the heat death) or excruciating torment for 1 googol to 10^10 googol years (until the heat death).

Argument 3. Benatar's asymmetry

The Basic Asymmetry

---

[55] Tomasik, Brian, How Much Direct Suffering Is Caused by Various Animal Foods?, Essays on Reducing Suffering, http://reducing-suffering.org/how-much-direct-suffering-is-caused-by-various-animal-foods/#Results

According to David Benatar (also see Fig 2.)[56]:

(1) For existing person, presence of pain is bad;

(2) For existing person, presence of pleasure is good;

(3) For the potential person who has never been brought into existence, absence of pain is a real advantage over presence of pain in case of (1);

(4) For the potential person who has never been brought into existence, the absence of pleasure is not a real disadvantage over the presence of pleasure in the case of (2) because that person cannot be deprived of pleasure because it was never brought into existence.

Prof Benatar's insight strikes me as a moral truth that is the most important in the history of humanity. And his *magnum opus*, Better Never to Have Been would be (at least should be) remembered as one of the most important literatures of the so-called human history.

Prof Benatar argued, because the presence of pleasure of those who exist is not advantage over the absence of pleasure of those who have never brought into existence, "as long as life contains some bad in it,

---

[56] Benatar, David, Better Never to Have Been, Chapter 2, I slightly rephrased for easier understanding by comparison of (1) v. (3) and (2) v. (4) with p.14 of the Better Never …

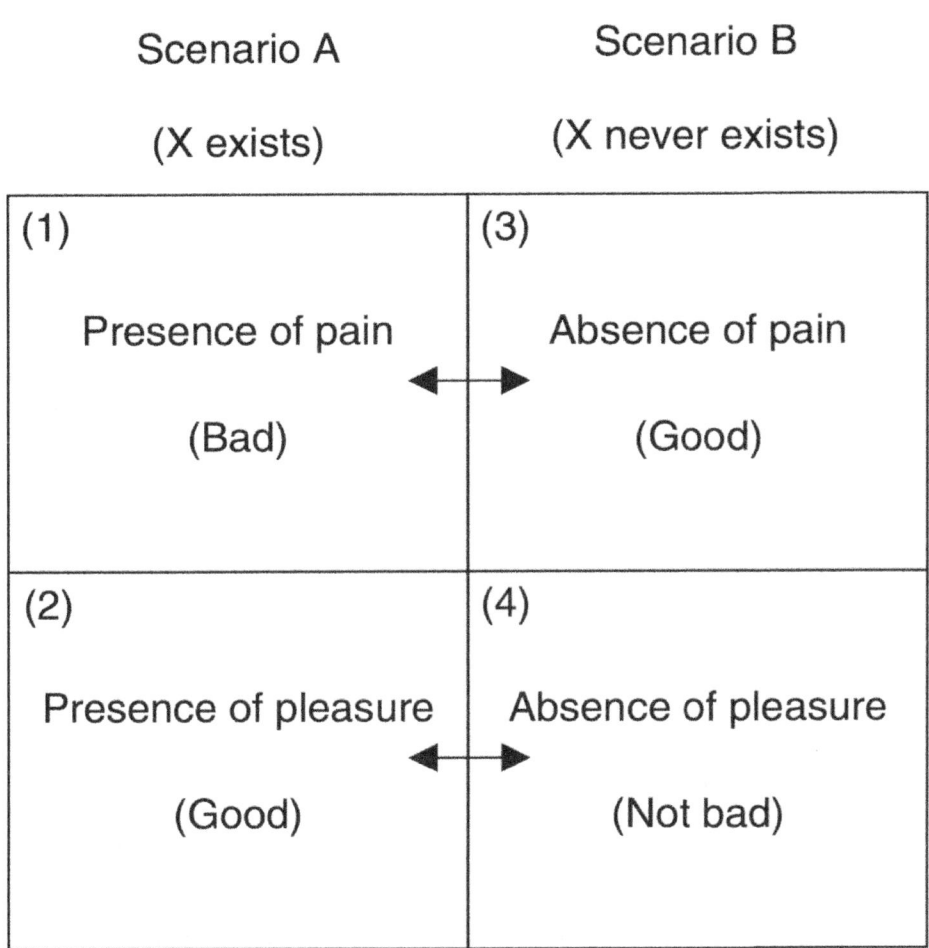

Fig. 2 (See footnote 56)

there is a net harm in coming into existence"[57]. Prof Benatar suggested that if there's no pain at all in life, coming into existence is neither harm nor benefit.

---

[57] Benatar, David, Paulson, Steve, The Harm of Coming Into Existence, To The Best of Our Knowledge, Wisconsin Public Radio, http://www.ttbook.org/listen/85221

From the axiological asymmetry above (which Prof Benatar named, the basic asymmetry[58]), Prof Benatar derived 4 other similar asymmetries.

Benatar's Four Other Asymmetries[59]

"i) The asymmetry of procreational duties:

While we have a duty to avoid bringing into existence people who would lead miserable lives, we have no duty to bring into existence those who would lead happy lives.

ii) The prospective beneficence asymmetry:

It is strange to cite as a reason for having a child that that child will thereby be benefited. It is not similarly strange to cite as a reason for not having a child that that child will suffer.

iii) The retrospective beneficence asymmetry:

When one has brought a suffering child into existence, it makes sense to regret having brought that child into existence – and to regret it for the sake of that child. By contrast, when one fails to bring a happy child into existence, one cannot regret that failure for the sake of the person.

---

[58] Benatar, David. "Still better never to have been: a reply to (more of) my critics." The Journal of ethics 17.1-2 (2013): p. 123.

[59] Ibid.

iv) The asymmetry of distant suffering and absent happy people:

We are rightly sad for distant people who suffer. By contrast we need not shed any tears for absent happy people on uninhabited planets, or uninhabited islands or other regions on our own planet."

Augmented asymmetry: why procreation is always a harm even if there's no suffering

Here I shall argue, that it is unethical to bring a sentient being into sentient existence even if the sentience would continue eternally without annihilation, and there's no pain at all in any degree whatsoever in any moment of sentient existence, and that sentient being would enjoy the best cognitively possible pleasure possible for the level of technology of that moment. The reason is simple. All sentient being that was brought into sentient existence can be deprived of pleasures. And all sentient being can enjoy pleasure infinite intensity in any given moment. Therefore, the sentient being enjoying the finite intensity of pleasure at any given moment is deprived of the infinite amount of pleasure compared to the hypothetical infinite intensity of pleasure.

The objection that hypothetically infinite pleasure is impossible

Of course, there can be an objection that hypothetically infinite pleasure is not actually possible. But even if in that case, we can compare the pleasure any sentient being enjoying in any given moment with say, the pleasure intensity that is the double of the pleasure intensity of the former.

If there are two immortal species without any suffering, but one has pleasure minimal intensity of pleasure 1 second a day and another has intense pleasure for 24 hours per day, we would and should think that the latter is immensely better than the former, and the former is immensely worse than the latter.

Negative Utilitarianism

Negative Utilitarianism is the idea that reduction of pain is morally important or urgent than increasing pleasure. The term humanitarian crisis itself strongly implies that what is morally urgent is the reduction of suffering, not the increase of pleasure. Corollary of Negative Utilitarianism is obviously assignment of negative value to procreation (anti-natalism).

But it does not follow all negative utilitarians should be a proscriptive/ prescriptive or moral/ethical anti-natalist. That is to say, even those who think that coming into existence is a (serious) harm (descriptive/

axiological anti-natalist) may think (human) procreation may be conducive to reduce the total amount of suffering in the world. Brian Tomasik suggested in his article that although it is true a person is harmed by coming into existence, reduction of wild animal population (according to Living Planet Index, the wild animal population was halved compared to 1970[60]) because of the existence of the human race reduced the total amount of suffering in the planet.[61] Negative Utilitarian David Pearce pointed out non-procreation of anti-natalists creates selection pressure for pro-natalism.[62]

Argument 4. Consent

Lack of consent of the child

Lack of capacity to give informed consent do not automatically mean it is ethical or legal to subjecting somebody to the certain action, as we can see, for example, the age of consent law (statutory rape law).

---

[60] Living Planet Index, Zoological Society of London and WWF, 2014, http://www.livingplanetindex.org/projects?main_page_project=LivingPlanetReport&home_flag=1

[61] Tomasik, Brian, Strategic Considerations for Moral Antinatalists, Essays on Reducing Suffering, http://reducing-suffering.org/strategic-considerations-moral-antinatalists/

[62] Pearce, David, 2007, Review: Better Never To Have Been: the harm of coming into existence by David Benatar, https://www.abolitionist.com/anti-natalism.html

Jimmy A. Licon's consent argument on the immorality of procreation[63]:

1. An individual is justified in subjecting someone to potential harm only if either: (a) they provide informed consent, (b) such is in their best interests, or (c) they deserve to be subjected to potential harm.
2. Bringing someone into existence is potentially subjecting them to harm.
3. Individuals that do not exist: (a) cannot give their consent to being brought into existence, (b) do not have interests to protect, and (c) do not deserve anything.
4. Hence, procreation is not morally justified."

Moreover, procreation is conducted non-consensually and also unsolicitedly (usually said by children to their parents "I never asked to be born").

Consent is the fundamental principle in the jurisprudence of all jurisdictions. Whereas potential (nonexistent) person lacks the capacity to give consent pertaining to procreation thereof, lack of capacity to give consent do not automatically deem the person given consent. It should be

---

[63] Licon, Jimmy Alfonso, Think, Volume 11 / Issue 32 / Autumn 2012, p. 88, Cambridge, The Royal Institute of Philosophy, 2012

always the best interest of the person, to be justified the action on him, if he lacks the capacity to give consent thereto.

For example, statutory rape is deemed illegal because the child (under the age of consent) deemed to lack the capacity to give consent, even if she has given (inadmissible) consent. Because a nonexistent person cannot have any interest to be brought into existence, it is not the best interest of the child to be brought into existence. Therefore, any procreation should be deemed illegal insofar the same legal principle applied to statutory rape/age of consent law.

It is curious why the principle of the best interests of the child do not apply to procreation whereas it does apply to adoption.
Indeed, adoption requires a lot of qualifications and safeguards to protect the child, including the economic ability of the prospective adoptive parents. Indeed, there're a lot of parents who would not qualify as adoptive parents for the reasons including economic ability go ahead recklessly procreating, without a shadow of guilt to children thereby victimised.

Unsolicitedness of life (life as an unsolicited gift)

Whereas the concept of 'solicitation' apparently commensurates with the concept of 'consent', the term 'unsolicited' apply even in the case of the person have the capacity to give consent.

A lot of children say to the parents thereof, "I was not asked to be born". Although it might be a difficult term for them the term 'unsolicited' perfectly and concisely describe the ultimate unsolicitedness (the very fact we were not asked to be born) of life.

Right to cognitive self-determination (cognitive liberty)

"Procreation is an act far more authoritarian than killing; and just as one should not take the life of someone else, one should also not impose life on someone else."

-Giovanni Soriano

One of the reason murder is considered wrong and criminalised in every competent jurisdiction is because it is a violation of the right to life, but also the ultimate violation of cognitive liberty. Because procreation is non-consensual and unsolicited infliction of sentience to (potential) sentient being, it could be also described as (one of) the ultimate violation of cognitive liberty.

Right to ontological self-determination (ontological liberty)

Similarly, procreation is a violation the right to ontological self-determination. Whereas murder violates only the ontological preference to (continue) to exist, procreation violates the right to ontological self-determination not to come into existence, and not to involuntarily cease to exist. (as shown above, the lack of the capacity to give consent of the person does not and should not mean ignorance of that person's best interest)

Retrospective Consent

Prospective (biological) parents may (wishfully and selfishly) think that their offspring may retrospectively consent for their decision for procreating their offspring. This argument is problematic in a lot of ways. First, obviously, not all people retrospectively consent to the parental decision to procreate them. Anti-natalists, obviously, do not give such retrospective consent. Also, as David Benatar pointed out, such retrospective consent may be hugely affected by 'adaptive preference'[64].

---

[64] Benatar, David, Fox, Rebecca, Better Never To Have Been: An Interview with David Benatar, Reasonable Vegan Network, Apr 17, 2016, rvgn.org/2016/04/17/better-never-to-have-been-an-interview-with-david-benatar/

Although one can commit suicide if he or she wanted, one cannot change the fact one has been born. Because the person can never change the fact one has been born, it is much more psychologically comforting to think one is benefited, and not at all harmed to be born. Adaptive preference can possibly apply to a lot of different things one cannot consent or voluntarily choose, such as, procreation, compulsory education, religious/ideological/nationalist/statist indoctrination, corporal punishment, circumcision, assigned gender, native language, one's parents, country of (natural born) citizenship, race, ethnic group, etc..

Jimmy Alfonso Licon argued, that people who attempt suicide may not have given retrospective consent to their procreation. He further argued "even if one of the partners having sex always consents after the action, this cannot justify the initial lack of consent. There are only a few cases where presumed consent is morally sufficient; assuming procreation is that sort of action begs the question. This is because the individual for whom consent is presumed has interests. Assisting an unconscious man in the absence of consent is morally acceptable given the man has interests worth preserving. That cannot be said of those who do not exist.".[65]

Prof Benatar argued that "The assumption that most people brought into existence will retrospectively consent to their creation is likely true. However, it does not justify our bringing children into existence. This is partly because we have reason to think that the preference of most people to have come into existence is an "adaptive preference" — a preference that people develop in order to cope with an unfortunate situation. When the infliction of harm causes the person harmed to come to consent to it, we should be very wary. If, for example, lobotomizing somebody caused that person to endorse the lobotomization, we would not – and should not – think that the retrospective consent justifies the practice."[66]

It should be noted, even if we think retrospective consent justifies the procreation, whereas no wrong could be done to the potential person one

---

[65] Licon, Jimmy Alfonso, Think, Volume 11 / Issue 32 / Autumn 2012, pp. 89-90, Cambridge, The Royal Institute of Philosophy, 2012

[66] Benatar, David, Fox, Rebecca, Better Never To Have Been: An Interview with David Benatar, Reasonable Vegan Network, Apr 17, 2016, rvgn.org/2016/04/17/better-never-to-have-been-an-interview-with-david-benatar/

failed to bring into existence, even if that person would be glad to be born if that person would be born, actual wrong is done to the person who have been brought into existence if that person retrospectively wish not to be born.[67]

Argument 5. Treating a child as an instrument

Procreation as an instrumentalisation of the child

There're documented cases of procreation to harvest organ, for example, bone mallow or a kidney to provide for one's child with a disease, for example, leukaemia or renal failure. Also in ordinary cases of procreation, the child cannot be brought into existence for its own sake (because the potential child is nonexistent, the nonexistent potential person cannot have any interest to come into existence). Prof Benatar argued, "In ordinary reproduction, people produce children (a) to satisfy their procreative or parenting interests; (b) to provide siblings to existing children; (c) to propagate the species, nation, tribe, or family; or (d) for no reason at all.", and therefore, ordinary procreation is more morally

---

[67] It is related to David Benatar's 'the asymmetry of procreational duties', see Chapter 1, Argument 3, Benatar's Four Other Asymmetries

problematic than procreation to save a life, because those reasons are weaker reasons of procreation than procreation for saving a life.[68]

Children are usually brought into existence for companion animal purposes. (to satisfy their procreative or parenting interests)[69]

Instrumentalisation as violation of human dignity

German Federal Constitutional Court stated striking down Section 14.3 of Aviation Security Act which enabled German Air Force to strike down hijacked airplane for the reason it was violation (unconstitutional) of human dignity clause of Article 1 of the Basic Law for the Federal Republic of Germany: "human dignity forbids the public authorities to use human beings as objects of their action, and as a mere means for the salvation of others. When the authorities use the death of innocent and helpless people to save other individuals, the former are being

---

[68] Benatar, David, Better Never to Have Been, pp. 130-131

[69] Ibid.

transformed into objects. And this neglects the constitutional status of the individuals as subjects with inherent dignity and inalienable rights."[70]

Procreation is essentially treating the future person as a mere mean and as an object (i.e. exploitation), as shown in the paragraph above 'procreation as instrumentalisation of the child'. Combined with German Constitutional Court's view that treating people as mere means is a violation of human dignity, procreation is a violation of, and not consistent with, human dignity. (Article 1 of the Universal Declaration of Human Rights, Article 1 of the Basic Law for the Federal Republic of Germany, Article 1 of the Charter of Fundamental Rights of the European Union) There're some cases parents have a baby to provide to get a suitable donor for its older sibling or another relative. There're parents who have a baby for marrow to provide for its sibling who has leukaemia, or even a kidney (one case)[71].

---

[70] Felipe, Miguel Beltran de, Santiago, Jose Maria Rodriguez de, Shooting Down Hijacked Airplanes? Sorry, We're Humanists. A Comment on the German Constitutional Court Decision of 2.15.2006, Regarding the Luftsicherheitsgesetz (2005 Air Security Act), ExpressO Preprint Series Year 2007 Paper 1983, https://www.unodc.org/tldb/pdf/EssayCivilAviation1.pdf

[71] The New York Times, More Babies Being Born to Be Donors of Tissue, 4 Jun 1991, http://www.nytimes.com/1991/06/04/health/more-babies-being-born-to-be-donors-of-tissue.html

Argument 6. Orphans

There are about 108 million orphans in the world.[72] By creating a new human, a couple is choosing to turn their face away from a young parentless child in the helpless situation who desperately need their help. It should be noted while adoption generally alleviates the suffering of the adopted child, procreation always inflicts suffering of the procreated child. (It should be noted there're a lot of moral corruptions in adoption 'industry', and the adopted child do not have a say as much as procreation)

Argument 7. Overpopulation and environment

Human population surpassed 1 billion in 1804. It took 123 years to add another 1 billion, in 1927. It took only 32 years human population grow to 3 billion in 1959, 15 years to 4 billion in 1974, 13 years to 5 billion in 1983, 12 years to 6 billion in 1999, 13 years to 7 billion in 2011.[73]

---

[72] https://en.wikipedia.org/wiki/Orphan#Populations

[73] https://en.wikipedia.org/wiki/World_population#Milestones_by_the_billions

It should be noted that poverty, unemployment and 'sweatshops' are partly caused by overpopulation. People in the developed countries procreating 1 child is essentially depriving the chance of a person in the developing countries to immigrate to richer countries. It would be needless to mention that procreation in the developed world depletes resources much more than procreation in developing the world.

Particularly those who is contemplating on procreation need to think about massive unemployment and uncertainty artificial intelligence will bring. Automation is already playing the huge role in unemployment. A lot of poor countries have fertility rate much higher than replacement, even though they can not feed and educate existing children and adults. Teacher-student ratio is very high in the poor countries, which result in the poorly educated new generation of that country.

It is needless to mention all anthropogenic climate change is attributable to procreation. According to Oregon State University, an American can only save 488 metric tonnes of carbon dioxide by all measures ("driving a high mileage car, recycling, or using energy-efficient appliances and light bulbs") combined. But if an American choose not to have one child he or she can reduce 9,441 metric tonnes of carbon footprint.[74] (it should be noted that this reduction is a co-reduction with the person's partner)

Argument 8. Animal holocaust

Although it may be possible that life of one self-aware sentient being is more valuable than one non-self-aware sentient being, there's no intrinsic reason to think the life of one self-aware sentient being is more valuable than two non-self-aware sentient being. For example, there's no intrinsic reason to think one human life is more valuable than two insect life. Perhaps there're more objective reasons to think that two insect life is more valuable than one human life.

Average Americans eat 16,000 animals in the course of their life.[75] It is estimated 166 billion animals are killed for human consumption every year.[76] Human animal devouring of non-human animals is particularly

---

[74] Family planning: A major environmental emphasis, Oregon State University, Jul 31, 2009 http://oregonstate.edu/ua/ncs/archives/2009/jul/family-planning-major-environmental-emphasis

[75] http://vegetariancalculator.com/vegetarian-calculator-yearly, https://en.wikipedia.org/wiki/List_of_countries_by_life_expectancy#List_by_the_World_Health_Organization_.282015.29, this calculation used US life expectancy of 79.3 years

[76] Benatar, David, Wasserman, David, Debating Procreation, p. 93

culpable in a way predation by wild animal is not. Of course, the majority of human have intelligence to contemplate on animal-eating. But another important difference is that we are the only species that breed and raise animals to eat. No totalitarian countries are known to breed and raise millions of human for consumption of human flesh. Considering we have killed trillions of animals for pleasure in the animal concentration-annihilation camp ('factory farm'), and particularly by intentionally breeding and raising for the sole purpose of exploitation is enough to be described "absurd and evil"[77], "patently evil"[78] or "animal holocaust is far worse than any crime committed against the human race"[79][80].

Prospective parents who're vegans have an excellent reason not to bring their potential children into existence, as they cannot ensure their offspring would be vegan when grown up.

Argument 9. (Un)aesthetic

---

[77] Benatar, David, The Species Barrier 35 Antinatal, Oct 9th, 2015, 0:33, http://thespeciesbarrier.podbean.com/e/the-species-barrier-35-antinatal/

[78] Ibid.

[79] Mistro, The Species Barrier 35 Antinatal, Oct 9th, 2015, 0:49, http://thespeciesbarrier.podbean.com/e/the-species-barrier-35-antinatal/

[80] see https://en.wikipedia.org/wiki/Animal_rights_and_the_Holocaust

"We are born between faeces and urine." -St Augustine

"[H]ow many more producers of excrement and urine, flatulence, menstrual blood and semen, sweat, mucus, vomit, and pus do we really need?" -David Benatar

David Benatar provided (un)aesthetic considerations for anti-natalism. According to his calculation, "[o]ver the course of a lifetime, the average person excretes approximately 50,969 liters of urines and more than 2467 kg of feces". Other (un)aesthetic considerations he provided include, "olfactory repugnance" (which require deodorisation), "[s]tatistical abnormal"ity of "physical beauty", littering, noise, "fumes from factories, cars, and cigarettes", and "masses of rubbish"[81]

Chapter 2. Anti-natalist activism

Contraception

About 38% of all pregnancies are estimated to be unintended in the world, resulting in 33 million unintended births annually, which is about a quarter of estimated about 135 million births. Contraception is failing in

---

[81] Benatar, David, et al., Permissible Progeny?: The Morality of Procreation and Parenting, Oxford University Press, 2015, Chapter 1. The Misanthropic Argument for Anti-natalism, From the Bad to the Ugly: (Un)aesthetic Considerations

too many cases. "Among unintended pregnancies in the United States, 60% of the women used birth control to some extent during the month pregnancy occurred."[82] More reliable, yet not perfect methods of contraception, such as vasectomy or tubal ligation (particularly, vasectomy) are unpopular among young people because they want to have children, doctors are reluctant to sterilise young, or have a myth that vasectomy will lower their libido.

Alternative entertainment methods

Some studies suggested that televisions reduce the fertility rate[83]. By developing more alternative entertainment methods, including, television, VOD service, video games, virtual reality, etc. we can reduce fertility rate. The alternative entertainment might be even addressed to the alternative relief of sexual desires, including pornographies, VR-based pornographies, cybersex, sexual partner robot, etc.

Non-human animal companion animal/robot

---

[82] https://en.wikipedia.org/wiki/Pregnancy

[83] Why aren't there more babies? Cable TV access reduces fertility rates, Guardian, Dec 10, 2014, https://www.theguardian.com/money/2014/dec/10/why-arent-there-more-babies-us-fertility-rate-declines-economists-baffled

A lot of people procreate for human companion animal purposes. We could encourage adoption (but not breeding) of abandoned non-human animals, thereby reducing demand for companion human animals. Of course, demand for companion human animals can be met by adoption as well. Also, robots equipped with AI can serve as a companion robot, thereby reducing the urge to procreate for human companion animal purposes.

Girls' education, prosperity

More educated girls have fewer children.[84] Among the reasons are 1) more knowledge on contraception/family planning 2) more prudence in procreative decision 3) more likeliness to engage in paid employment, instead of becoming a full-time housewife. 4) married at the older age 5) more empowered to decide number of babies for her interest, possibly against pressure from husband, parents, parents-in-law and community 6) lower teenage pregnancy rate 7) less likely to be sexually active at young age

---

[84] https://www.weforum.org/agenda/2015/11/the-relationship-between-womens-education-and-fertility/

Japan, South Korea, Hong Kong, Taiwan, Macau, Singapore all have very low fertility rate, below replacement, 1.40, 1.25, 1.18, 1.12, 0.94, 0.81, respectively.[85] In these regions, girls and women who are 15 to 34 are highly educated, a lot of them had tertiary educations, perhaps even more than boys and men. Teenage pregnancy rate in these regions is among the lowest in the world.

Prosperity and education in general

Prosperity and education, in general, lower fertility rate.[86][87] As economy become more advanced, it needs more quality than quantity, so economic value of children can be increased by having fewer children and concentrating resources. Also, prosperity provides easier access to contraception, sterilisation, alternative entertainments. Also, the society becomes more individualistic and tolerant as it becomes richer, thereby reducing family/relative/community pressure to 'continue' family or tribe, to marry and have a lot of kids.

---

[85] https://en.wikipedia.org/wiki/List_of_sovereign_states_and_dependent_territories_by_fertility_rate

[86] https://en.wikipedia.org/wiki/Income_and_fertility

[87] https://en.wikipedia.org/wiki/Fertility_and_intelligence#Education

I would not be surprised that research found out anti-natalists, child-free people, vegans have above average education/intelligence/ socioeconomic status. Particularly, religious people can rarely become an anti-natalist, anti-natalism requires further intelligence than becoming not religious (Agnostic/Atheist). Indeed, high degree (possibly very high degree) of intellect is a prerequisite to understanding arguments of anti-natalism.

Vegans/Animal Rights activists

A lot of vegans opposes breeding of non-human animals. A lot of vegans realise they are preventing factory farmed animals brought into existence, instead of saving lives.[88] (Of course, for wild fishes, vegans are saving their lives) It is curious only a few of vegans and animal rights advocate seemed to realise their opposition to non-human animal breeding can be extended to human animal as well. At least as much as breeding of non-human animal cannot be justified because of there're a lot of abandoned non-human animals, insofar there're abandoned human animal children who need adoptive parents, breeding cannot be justified.

---

[88] Benatar, David, Fox, Rebecca, Better Never To Have Been: An Interview with David Benatar, Reasonable Vegan Network, Apr 17, 2016, rvgn.org/2016/04/17/better-never-to-have-been-an-interview-with-david-benatar/

It should be also noted that breeding of human animal for companion animal purposes (pet, i.e. human animal child-rearing experience) or economic purposes (for child labor or as a 'pension' or 'insurance', particularly after old age) is exploitive and morally problematic, at least as much as breeding non-human animal for the pet purposes or economic purposes (factory farming of non-human animals). Also, it's very unlikely none of vegan biological parents' descendants does not consume any animal products. Because veganism is hard to do, chances are there would be more than one person who consumes animal products among vegan's children, grandchildren and numerous descendants of innumerous generations thereafter.

Considering popularity of veganism, and considering about 1% to 2% of the population of developed world is vegan (minority but big number and impact considering population of developed world) it would be completely possible to further anti-natalist movements (right not to be born/anti-natal right movements) to the level of animal rights movements or LGBT movements, furthermore, (slavery) abolition movements and/or women's suffrage movements, African's rights movement.

Kantians and deontologists

Kantians, although it's doubtful how many people will identify themselves so, can be anti-natalists as well, since procreation is essentially treating the resultant child as mere means to serve parental or other interests.

Child rights activists

It can be considered a violation of child right to procreate, and therefore, child rights activists can be anti-natalists.

Existing anti-natalist movements

There are existing (population) anti-natalist movements. For example, Population Action International (PAI), Population Matters, World Vasectomy Day all have the view the world have human overpopulation (or we would soon have the human overpopulation), and try to address the overpopulation by the reduction of the fertility rate.

Although leaning toward choice-natalist view (reproductive freedom view) than anti-natalist view (procreation reduction or abolition), Planned Parenthood or United Nations Population Fund can be seen as somewhat anti-natalist.

Chapter 3. Anti-natalist policy

Universal Declaration of Human Rights

Article 16, Paragraph 1 of the Universal Declaration of Human Rights stipulates, "Men and women of full age, without any limitation due to race, nationality or religion, have the right to marry and to found a family.". The right 'to found a family' "is clearly intended and understood that the right includes the procreative founding of a family."[89]

Rome Statute of the International Criminal Court

Article 6 (d) and Article 7, Paragraph 1 (g) of the Rome Statute of the International Criminal Court criminalised "Imposing measures intended to prevent births within the group;" and "enforced sterilization" as a genocide and a crime against humanity respectively. Article 7, Paragraph 1 (k) "Other inhumane acts of a similar character intentionally causing great suffering or serious injury to body or to mental or physical health." can also be interpreted to prohibit national jurisdiction's non-discriminatory prohibition of procreation by means not involving enforced sterilisation (by punishment (e.g. incarceration, fine) conforming to international standards, i.e. neither cruel nor unusual)

---

[89] Benatar, David, Better Never to Have Been, p. 102

Natural-born-citizen clause of the US Constitution

Natural-born-citizen clause of Article 2, Section 1, clause 5 of the Constitution of the United States can be interpreted to imply non-prohibition (if not the treatment of procreation as a natural right) of procreation within the jurisdiction thereof.

Impunity and immunity for procreative infliction of death and other harms

Harm	Infliction of harm by procreation	Infliction of harm by non-procreative ways (on human animals)
Death	Legal	Illegal
Pain	Legal	Illegal
Disability	Legal	Illegal

We've seen that procreative infliction of death can be as harmful as a non-procreative infliction of death, if not more harmful. And it is obvious that procreative infliction of death (i.e. procreation) is treated with impunity. I shall discuss the impunity for procreative infliction of death (i.e. procreation) and the possibility and implications of the prohibition of procreative infliction of death (i.e. procreation).

Obviously, no competent jurisdiction have adopted general prohibition of procreation. There have been limited anti-natal policies such as China's former one-child policy, but China's one-child policy is "a response to massive (rather than merely moderate) overpopulation"[90] and also do not prohibit all procreation (i.e. permit the procreation of the one's first child). In cases of "measures intended to prevent births within the group" for eugenics or racist purposes, obviously 'desirable' procreations are not prohibited, if not encouraged.

Of course, there's an English common law principle of the year and a day rule, or the three years and a day rule for the State of California, but even if death happen on or before one or three years after the birth or sexual contact resulted birth, parents are not criminally liable for the death of the child.

Although Article 16, Paragraph 1 of the Universal Declaration of the Human Rights stipulates the right to 'found a family', the right to 'found a family' understood as a right to procreate seems to be inconsistent with human dignity (Article 1), right to life (Article 3, because procreation is (the ultimate) cause of death), social and international order for protection of human rights (Article 28) and prohibition of destruction of rights (Article 30).

---

[90] Ibid., p. 12

Preamble of the Rome Statute says the purpose of the Statute and establishment of the ICC-CPI is to end impunity for international crimes (subject to jurisdiction thereof), "Determined to put an end to impunity for the perpetrators of these crimes and thus to contribute to the prevention of such crimes,"

If we should think not just the practices of murder, lynching, slavery, female genital mutilation, etc. themselves but also (even if non-discriminatory) impunity and/or governmental aiding and abetting of such practices as human right violations, why not just practice of procreation themselves but impunity and/or governmental aiding and abetting (pro-natal policies, e.g. paid maternity leaves, welfare benefit for people having children, etc.) of procreation (which invariably includes procreative infliction of sentience, pain and death) also a violation of human right?

Of course, this is not to insist a prohibition of procreation or mass sterilisation program should be introduced. That's not just because the former is very likely, and the latter is certainly prohibited by the Rome Statute of the International Criminal Court. As Prof Benatar argued, there can be good reasons to legally allow people to do wrong things, even if some action is morally wrong.[91] Prohibition of procreation is likely to increase suffering in the world, rather than reduce it.[92]

Procreation as a tort (wrongful life cause of action)

"Wrongful life is the name given to a legal action in which someone is sued by a severely disabled child (through the child's legal guardian) for failing to prevent the child's birth.

Now this should be extended to the wrongful imposition of sentience. So all those who claim they have had sentience wrongfully imposed upon them should be compensated by their parents and by the State. This would be subject to them not having procreated themselves and to voluntarily being sterilized.

The compensation could be a monthly allowance or a lump sum or various benefits in kind. It should be sufficient to provide them with a reasonable quality of life.

In many other areas people are compensated for such things as medical negligence, rape, grievous bodily harm, murder of relatives, riots, civil commotion etc., so why not here."

---

[91] Ibid. p. 103

[92] Benatar, David, Wasserman, David, Debating Procreation, pp. 14-15

-Existential Depression, Facebook page[93]

Even if we do not (and I think we should not) criminalise procreation, anti-natalist view on procreation may imply that children should have the right to require compensation for the tort of wrongful infliction of sentience to one's (biological) parents and physicians who assisted one's conception (if procreation is aided by doctors, e.g. by in-vitro-fertilisation). Because it is parents who're indebted to children, not vice versa, children should have more claim than one's spouse to require the portion of parents' property. The most importantly, because children's association with their parents is involuntary, children should have more claim than voluntary spouses of usual cases of voluntary marriage.

Procreation tax

To procreate can be understood as voting for pro-natalist policies (encouragement, endorsement or permission of procreation). Therefore, all procreators are collectively responsible for the poverty in pro-natalist

---

[93] Existential Depression, Facebook page, https://www.facebook.com/permalink.php?story_fbid=468086643296211&id=229835853787959, 18 Jan 2014

society. (since procreation is "the root of all evil"[94], poverty is also procreativity caused) Therefore, there could be a 'procreation tax' policy like 'meat tax' or 'sin tax'. 'Procreation tax' could be imposed as a lump sum, or imposed as a form of a surtax on the income tax. (it may be possible only procreators and non-vegans are liable for tax)

For example, procreation tax can be imposed as an income tax, with the tax rate of 30% of the annual income for the person with one child, 50% for the person with two children, 70% for the person with three children or more. By only taxing people who procreate (or procreated), we can realise libertarians' ideal, taxation-optional society. Of course, there are a lot of implications of the procreation tax. Procreation tax may incentivise progenitors to hide that they are procreating or have children. More parturition can happen at the home, instead of a hospital, thereby endangering pregnant women and the foetus/neonate. Particularly, progenitors may not declare and register the birth of the child to the government, thereby denying the child of the education, protection (from parental and other abuse), citizenship and government-issued ID.

---

[94] Benatar, David, Attia, Guillaume A.W., Why We Should Stop Reproducing, The Critique, Sep 21, 2015, http://www.thecritique.com/articles/why-we-should-stop-reproducing-an-interview-with-david-benatar-on-anti-natalism/

Procreation tax usage for universal basic income

Procreation tax can be used as a source of universal basic income. Such basic income can be paid for only people who do not have children, or even only for people who have got a sterilisation. Because life is an unsolicited thing, it is unfair to impose work obligation only to survive (to procrastinate death for a few decades) for those who do not impose life on one's offspring. Furthermore, the basic income can be paid only for people who are vegan, alongside sterilised and/or anti-natalist.

Procreation tax usage for universal cryonics

Because life was unsolicitedly and non-consensually imposed on the victim (of the procreation), the progenitors (perpetrators) of the victim of the procreation have the moral obligation to support their children for the entire life and provide the access to the transhumanist life extension, such as a cryonics.

Cryonics can be subsidised by the procreation tax, of which all people are cryopreserved if they wanted, or all people who never procreated are cryopreserved if they wanted.

Children's rights

Anti-natalist view may also suggest requirement of higher level of support of children, longer duration of support beyond age e.g. 18 or 21, (as good as the child's parents reasonably do), increased protection of children's right (e.g. prohibition of cruel and unusual punishment such as some or all cases of corporal punishment), increased freedom of children to use their time and to choose their education and career (and requirement of support even if child's parent don't like children's career choice), and emancipation of minor law more favourable to the child.

State discouragement of procreation

It may imply even if procreation is not criminalised, contraception, sterilisation, and abortion should be not just legal but also encouraged (by campaign) and subsidised (e.g. free vasectomy, free IUDs, free contraceptives, free abortion for pregnant poor women or pregnant teenage girl)

Chapter 4. Moral complexities

Is it immoral to save a life?: the negative externality of beneficence

Peter Singer provided 'Drowning Child Analogy' in his famous paper Famine, Affluence, and Morality (1972), that failure to save a geographically distant life by failure to donate can be as wrong as failure to save geographically near life (a drowning child).[95]

The basic idea of this chapter is simple. Even though we have a *prima facie* duty of beneficence (including the duty to a save life if one could), that *prima facie* duty of beneficence can be overridden if that beneficence may cause serious (harmful) side effect on other sentient beings. For example, saving a non-vegetarian human animal may cause that saved human animal eating thousands of non-human animals until his or her death, and then it may be desirable not to save that human animal's life in order to save thousands of non-human animals. (it does not follow we should kill that human animal)

Prima facie **duties**

According to W.D. Ross, we have a few *prima facie* duties that may override each other in certain circumstances.[96]

---

[95] https://en.wikipedia.org/wiki/Famine,_Affluence,_and_Morality, Singer, Peter (Spring 1972). "Famine, Affluence, and Morality". Philosophy and Public Affairs. Princeton University Press. 1 (3): 229–243. doi: 10.2307/2265052. JSTOR 2265052.

[96] W. D. Ross's Moral Theory, http://www.hu.mtu.edu/~tlockha/hu329ov8.htm, Garrett, Jan, A Simple and Usable (Although Incomplete) Ethical Theory Based on the Ethics of W. D. Ross, http://people.wku.edu/jan.garrett/ethics/rossethc.htm, 2004

1. Fidelity;

2. Reparation;

3. Gratitude;

4. Justice;

5. Beneficence;

6. Self-Improvement;

7. Non-maleficence (non-injury);

I would like to augment W.D. Ross' 7 duties with the (*prima facie*) duty of side-effect prevention (or duty of precaution). Although the duty of side effect prevention may be included in the duty of non-maleficence, I think it is desirable to separate it from the duty of non-injury. The duty of precaution may include, for example, the duty to prevent official development assistance (ODA) abused to continue poverty in the poor countries; the duty to ensure the alien the country admit is unlikely to pose danger to its nationals and residents; and the duty to prevent detrimental side effect certain technology (such as nuclear fission) would precipitate.

I shall argue, in practically all cases of beneficence (humanitarianism), the side effect is unavoidable. This is not to say such beneficence is unethical or undesirable, but to note the moral dilemma philanthropic, zoophilic and/or sentiophilic people (including the majority of effective altruists) nowadays are facing, and our potential offspring may have to face.

Procreative externality of saving life

Holocaust rescuer Sir Nicholas Winton saved 669 children, and about 7,000 people are estimated to alive because of him. I.e. at least about 6,000 people are procreated as a result of Sir Nicholas' rescue. Whereas 669 rescued people were already condemned to death by their progenitors, i.e. they will invariably die even if they were rescued, 6,000 resultant lineal descendants do not have to die at all if they were not born (if not Sir Nicholas' rescue).

Similar trolley problem-like moral dilemma present in almost all cases of saving potentially or actually fertile human (practically every human except post-menopausal women). For example, donation of $28 billion by Bill Gates are estimated to be saved 6 million people. Within just a few decades, it would result in the procreation of millions and millions of resultant descendants that will invariably die.

Carnistic[97] externality of saving life

Average human in the world eats more than one thousand animals in the course of their life. Average Americans eat 16,000 animals in the course of their life. Because a saving life of one non-vegetarian human animal has cost of thousands of animal lives, the person who would save a non-vegetarian human life would need justifications for doing so at the cost of animals.

That may include, (1) life in the imminent danger (duty of beneficence) have priority over potential and uncertain danger to life in the future (duty of side effect prevention); (2) moral duty toward genetically or socially close to us should have priority (toward family, friends, acquaintances, community, ethnic group, state, conspecifics); (3) human life is more valuable than thousands of non-human life; and (4) non-human animals do not have any moral standing and we can use them as we please.

---

[97] The term carnism was coined by Joy, Melanie, 2001, see https://en.wikipedia.org/wiki/Carnism and Joy, Melanie, Why We Love Dogs, Eat Pigs, and Wear Cows: An Introduction to Carnism, Conari Press, 2009

Whereas the practice of eating animals can be described as 'meat-eating', zoophagy or sentiophagy, but a conventional ideology on moral status, and our duty (at least, duty of non-maleficence) toward non-human sentient beings can be best described and defined carnism (see ibid. in this footnote)

Argument (4) is an appalling argument which can be described 'speciest'. Such view has been applied to women, children, people of minority race and followers of the minority religion. Argument (3) is more plausible than argument (4), but although it sounds plausible to think human life is more valuable than non-human animal life, it is very unclear how much weight we should give to humans. Most people may agree human life is not as valuable as one septillion (10^{24}) non-human animal life. It would be very speciest/anthropocentric to think so. While it may be easily agreeable that one human life is more valuable than one non-human animal life, the weight of human life may vary hugely. Some may think the multiplier should be 1.5, some may think 10, 100, 1000, 10000, 100000, 1 million. But there's no intrinsic reason the value of human life should be just above the number of animals he would eat during his life. If the multiplier could be 100000, why not one million, one billion, one trillion, one quadrillion, one septillion (10^{24}), or one googol (10^{100})?

The major views on axiology of human and non-human sentient beings' value of (sentient) life can be outlined as below. (1) human and non-human (sentient) life both have an infinite value; (2) human life have an infinite value, while non-human animals have a finite value; and (3) human life and non-human animal life both have a finite value. I shall argue, that view (2) should be rejected because it is speciest/ anthropocentric. View (3) require us to think human life is at least about 20,000 times more valuable to justify saving a life, it is far from clear why we shouldn't think the multiplier is 200 or 2 septillion. View (1), the view I hold, is the only view that is compatible with the idea of 'intrinsic and inviolable dignity of all sentient beings'. But it would require us to think the value of one human life, seven billion human life, and one mosquito life the same, as they are all infinite. It could justify not killing one mosquito at the cost of two human dies from malaria as much as it could justify saving one life at the cost of thousands of non-human animals.

Argument (2) may also be speciest. Although it is true we allow some favouritism to some extent, we would not (and should not) think that a nation saving a life of 1 citizen at the cost of 1,000 foreigners is justified. It is as much far from clear we have the right to favour 1 conspecific at the cost of 1,000 fellow non-human animals.

Argument (1) seems to be the only plausible argument to defend saving human life at the cost of risking thousands of non-human animals. But it is far from clear we would also save one human at the imminent danger at the cost of risking thousands of humans.

Carnistic externality of poverty alleviation

'Meat' consumption per capita in South Korea 9-folded after 1970, and 'meat' consumption per capita in China 5-folded after 1982. It is more far from clear alleviation of poverty (suffering) of one human animal is justified at the cost of life and suffering of thousands of non-human animals than saving human life at the cost of lives of thousands of animals.

Philanthropic exploitation of non-human animals

The best example of philanthropic exploitation of non-human animals is, of course, animal exploitation, although many experiments are conducted for frivolous reasons. (this is not to say experimentation is justified if 'necessary') Many vegans or 'vegetarian' people seemingly are not aware that a lot of poorest human animals make living by animal exploitation. For example, in agriculture-based poor countries, people often procreate a lot of children to exploit them in the farm. Farms in the developing countries almost certainly use 'pest'icide or 'livestocks' such as a cow. A lot of people in poor countries make living by fishing. Bill Gates announced his plan to 'donate' more than 100,000 chickens for poverty alleviation in the poor countries.[98]

Unavoidable harms to non-human animals by even vegans

Even a vegan kill several vertebrates per year by crop cultivation, roadkill etc.. The number of killed animals by vegans may be thousands if insects killed by pesticide included. Also in this deeply interdependent economy, it is practically impossible for vegans not to patronise animal exploitation. By taxation, consumption, donation and etc. (e.g. gov't grant to animal experimentation, food stamp to non-vegan food, etc.) vegans indirectly patronise breeding of non-human animal for exploitation. Although death by starvation for ethical reasons (to not to patronise killing of any animals, even by crop cultivation or taxation) may cause immense amount of suffering to family and friends, a decision to eat vegan food instead of fasting oneself to death is a choice based more on duty of self-improvement than strict adherence to duty of non-maleficence (if bereavement caused by starving to death is not considered non-maleficence).

---

[98] Gates, Bill, Jun 7, 2016, Why I Would Raise Chickens, Gates Notes, https://www.gatesnotes.com/Development/Why-I-Would-Raise-Chickens

Moral Dilemmas in Anti-natalism Advocacy

For example, if one convince 1000 people not to procreate, and as a result of that, 200 couples break up because of disagreement on whether or not to procreate, 150 new couples may be formed with different match, if 100 out of 150 new couples marry and they have 2 children per couple, 200 people will be unsolicitedly-nonconsensually procreated with different genetic composition and their procreation will invariably result in death. I.e. even if one save 2000 potential people 'from life' by anti-natalism advocacy, 200 people may be brought into existence as a side-effect of such advocacy (similar problem with trolley problem), and such 200 victims of procreation are not 2,000 beneficiaries, because 200 victims have different genetic composition with 2000 beneficiaries (because one of the biological parents are different).

Furthermore, moral anti-natalist acting on anti-natalism by desisting from procreation is creating strong selection pressure for genetic or memetic tendency for pro-natalism among human animals, as David Pearce pointed out. Opting-out procreation may cause wild animal habitat recovery, thereby wild animal population may increase, and thereby indirectly cause immense amount of wild animal suffering.

Maleficence on the sentient being for the beneficence of the same sentient being

Sometimes, maleficence on the sentient being is required for the harm prevention or the conferral of the intrinsic good (upon the same sentient being). One good example may be a compulsory education. There is no doubt that compulsory education is effectively a kind of 'involuntary servitude'. It is far from clear whether we should describe compulsory education intended to prevent harm (of ignorance) or confer the good (of knowledge/education). It should be noted, however, that even if the benefit or harm prevention of the compulsory education outweigh the deprivation of liberty (involuntary servitude) and other harms or unpleasantness associated with compulsory education, the involuntary servitude (of up to 12 years) is *pro tanto* bad.

Advocates for compulsory education, particularly compulsory education as a 'human right', how much well-intentioned they are, advocating for the involuntary servitude, which is *pro tanto* maleficence and, violence.

(Here I should elaborate again that the ignorance progenitors impose upon their offspring so that purportedly necessitates involuntary servitude-education is completely gratuitous since they can simply desist from procreation not to create urgent need for the compulsory education)

Maleficence on the sentient being for the beneficence of the other sentient beings

There are cases which maleficence which may not qualify as exploitation of the sentient beings is required for the purported beneficence (more accurately, harm prevention) on the other sentient beings. For example, killing mosquito(s) possibly carrying malaria virus to purportedly protect human animals is one of such cases. One problem of universal justification of such violence which is purportedly intended to protect human animals is that it is implicitly assuming human animals are (far) more valuable than non-human animals. Even if human animal life is more valuable than non-human animal life, it does not follow the interest to preserve human animal life can override the interests to preserve non-human animal life.

If we have the right to use insecticide to kill insects that are potentially harmful to human animals, there is no intrinsic reason to think we are not allowed to use anthropocide to kill human animals (such as non-vegans) that are potentially (more likely, actually) (very) harmful to non-human animals. (of course, this is not to suggest killing (non-vegan) human animals, neither to say we should never use insecticide, but just to point out our moral selfishness for its own sake)

Impossibility of universal beneficence

Universal beneficence, which can be defined as beneficence on one or more sentient being while harming no sentient being, is *de facto* impossible. I have shown that even saving life and poverty alleviation have a substantial side effect on non-human animals. Even convincing others not to have children, or going vegetarian or vegan has substantial side effects, most notably possible increase of wild animal suffering by wild animal habitat preservation or recovery.

Although utilitarians may be unconcerned about (harmful) side effects, provided the benefit of the particular course of the action outweigh the (harmful) side effects, in this 'chaotic' cosmos in which the causal chain is so complex, it is impossible to tell whether particular course of action increase or decrease the amount of total suffering (disutility) (for negative utilitarians) or the amount of total utility (for classical utilitarians). Particularly, if a utilitarian think that a death (annihilation) also has some moral considerability, the objective axiology to convert annihilation of the sentience into a particular amount of disutility (physical pain and mental suffering) is impossible.

Professional duty and non-professional duty

It should be noted that professional duty may dictate a different course of action from what (non-professional, general) moral code dictates. For example, for people outside medical profession or people who are not rescue worker, et al., it may be desirable not to save Hitler's life (e.g. by CPR), or even it may be desirable not to save non-vegan's life (this is not to say it is desirable or permissible to kill Hitler's life or non-vegan's life). But for medical doctors, they may have a professional duty to save human life non-discriminatorily.[99]

Chapter 5. Miscellaneous

Pro-death view on abortion

David Benatar argued that combining anti-natalist view with pro-choice view on abortion would lead to what he calls 'pro-death view on abortion'. The view abortion is preferable before the fetus become sentient.[100]

---

[99] https://en.wikipedia.org/wiki/Declaration_of_Geneva#Declaration

[100] Benatar, David, Better Never to Have Been, Chapter 5

According to Royal College of Obstetricians and Gynecologists (2010), "In reviewing the neuroanatomical and physiological evidence in the fetus, it was apparent that connections from the periphery to the cortex are not intact before 24 weeks of gestation and, as most neuroscientists believe that the cortex is necessary for pain perception, it can be concluded that the fetus cannot experience pain in any sense prior to this gestation.".[101]

Non-human animal breeding

Breeding of non-human animals for the reasons such as exploitation for animal product production, animal experimentation, companion animal, etc. have exceptional culpability compared to wild animal hunting, because it creates an unnecessary annihilation of sentience, whereas wild animal hunting (such as wild fisheries) only makes annihilation happen sooner than later. Veganism (not just vegan diet but desisting from using animal products, and also desisting from breeding non-human animals) should be encouraged, if not required by the government.

---

[101] Royal College of Obstetricians and Gynecologists, Fetal Awareness – Review of Research and Recommendations for Practice, 2010, https://www.rcog.org.uk/globalassets/documents/guidelines/rcogfetalawarenesswpr0610.pdf

It is curious why (most of) vegans and animal rights advocates oppose breeding of non-human animals but not breeding of human animals. If breeding of non-human animals to exploit them as companion animals or economic purposes are wrong, breeding of human animals to exploit them as human companion animals or for economic purposes (which is quite the case in the developing world) are at least as morally problematic as breeding of non-human animals for such purposes.

Legal personhood of non-human sentient beings

Although so-called self-awareness or other so-called high level of cognition are important features of sentient existence, sentience itself, I think, is enough to qualify a sentient being for an individuality and a personhood as an individuality. Every sentient being is individual and final.[102] Because all sentient beings are individual and final, all sentient beings are persons. What I mean by that every sentient being is individual is, that the subjective phenomenal experience of individual sentient being cannot be felt by another (aside indirect influences of one's phenomenal experience toward another). That individuality of sentient beings also

---

[102] Gray, John N., The Silence of Animals: On Progress and Other Modern Myths, Penguin, 2013, "Humanity is a fiction composed from billions of individuals for each of whom life is singular and final."

applies to sentient beings' annihilation. And what I mean by that every sentient being is final is, that the annihilation of individual sentient being is final.

Although it has been suggested some sentient beings lack the personhood[103], the threshold for the personhood can be arbitrary, and such argument can be used as an argument for carnism.[104]

Legal personhood of pre-sentient sentient beings

Pre-sentient sentient beings are effectively disenfranchised of their legal personhood to be considered of their best interests, as non-human animals are disenfranchised of their legal personhood. In the principle of the best interest of the child, procreation is inconsistent with the principle of the best interest of the potential person, and therefore, procreation is not justifiable.

Possible dysgenic impact of anti-natalism

---

[103] https://en.wikipedia.org/wiki/Personhood

[104] Watch David Benatar, Jacques Rousseau, et al.'s debate, TEDxCapeTownSalon: Should Animals Be Off South African Menus? (Full version), Dec 2, 2014, Tedx Capetown, https://www.youtube.com/watch?v=IJYwN2X7IbI

It is likely people who acquaint the term anti-natalism (which is perhaps rarely known even by native speakers of English), and even act on it by desisting from procreation, or independently think that procreation may be morally problematic, may have much high IQ and/or moral goodness than the average.

If we recognise genetic or memetic heritability of intelligence, moral goodness, anti-natalism, veganism, it is true that anti-natalist acting on anti-natalism by desisting from procreation may create selection pressure for pro-natalism, carnism (the ideology that non-human animal (ab)use is acceptable) and moral egoism/selfishness.

It does not follow, however, that such so-called dysgenic impact is undesirable. Although it may be true that intelligence is an intrinsic good, it does not follow intelligence tends to reduce the overall amount of suffering of the sentient beings. It is true that higher intelligence gives stronger capacity to reduce suffering, but it is also true higher intelligence gives stronger capacity to inflict suffering. For example, 'meat' consumption per capita tends to be much larger in high-IQ, high-GDP per capita countries. Although human animals may be suffering less in high-IQ countries, and likely to have a higher prevalence of vegetarianism and veganism, carnists (people who think non-human animal ab(use) is acceptable) of high-IQ, high-GDP per capita countries have a much higher capacity to perpetrate non-human animals. And overall, 'meat' consumption apparently increased because of higher income in high-IQ countries is far larger than 'meat' consumption vegetarians in high-IQ countries reduced.[105]

A response to techno-optimists

Some transhumanists and techno-optimists suggested that technology may abolish death and suffering in the future. Of course, certainly, technology can possibly make coming into existence less bad. As technology so far achieved partial improvement (and partial deterioration). But I think there badness in birth (the initiation of sentience) that is not entirely reducible to the harmful side effects of the coming into existence (death and suffering)

For example, David Benatar recently argued the badness of death consists of the badness of annihilation and badness of deprivation. I.e. there's an intrinsic badness of death even if it will release the person from

---

[105] https://en.wikipedia.org/wiki/List_of_countries_by_meat_consumption, https://iq-research.info/en/page/average-iq-by-country

suffering, and give the person 'meaning', the person urgency, etc. I shall say we can and should think birth (the initiation of sentience) intrinsic bad. For example, if our government administer antidepressants in tab water without us knowing and without our consent, we would and should think it is wrong. Not just because it's side effects (possibly, reduction of discontent toward government, side effect of antidepressants) but also it's intrinsic badness (violation of people's (cognitive) liberty)

I think the same thing can be said for procreation like medicating antidepressants without consent is bad, even if it do not harm and only benefits the person. (Non-consensual and unsolicited) procreation is a violation of (ontological and cognitive) liberty. One is deprived of ontological and cognitive self-determination. Although it is true that pre-vital nonexistence is objectively nonexistence, subjectively, pre-vital nonexistence is neither subjective nonexistence nor subjective existence. Contrary to the pre-vital nonexistence, post-mortem nonexistence is somewhat subjectively non-existence. Although post-mortem nonexistent person does not have any subjective phenomenal experience to experience the nonexistence, post-mortem nonexistent person was used to exist.

Also, we do not know right now what kind of fate technology would lead us. As much as probability of salvation (abolition of suffering & death), there's non-negligible risk of annihilation, damnation, and anthropophagy.

Furthermore, we can not procreate in the hope technology may abolish death; as we can not procreate or kill somebody in the hope there would be an afterlife (which majority of humans seems to be believing). We should err on the side of the caution (precautionary principle) on whether or not technology will abolish suffering or whether or not there is an afterlife.

Asymmetry in our capacity to reduce and inflict suffering

There is apparently a crucial asymmetry in our capacity to reduce suffering and inflict suffering. An injury is quick, recovery is slow.[106] Killing a life is quicker, cheaper, and take less expertise than saving a life. Whereas all sentient beings can be killed, only sentient beings under immediate jeopardy of death can be saved. Even if we save a life, that life would invariably die within a few decades. Aside cryonics and possibility of the future abolition of death, 'saving a life' in fact only extend life for a few decades, and procrastinate death for a few decades.

---

[106] Benatar, David, Wasserman, David, Debating Procreation, p. 49

Particularly, whereas we can alleviate or prevent suffering of currently existing sentient beings or future sentient beings (which would come into existence if we do not intervene), we can inflict suffering not just on currently existing sentient beings or future sentient beings (which would come into existence if we do not intervene) but also we are capable of creating more sentient beings to inflict suffering upon. We are actually creating billions of human and non-human animals for the selfish reasons (i.e. exploitation), effectively inflicting an immense amount of suffering upon them, even if the infliction of suffering is not intentional and it may not necessarily involve malice aforethought (it depends on how you define intention and malice aforethought).

If nematodes are sentient, it is estimated that there is 10^{22} (10 sextillions) sentient beings on this planet.[107] The best possible scenario of technological singularity can only alleviate the current suffering of 10^{22} sentient beings (of course, this assumes that only this planet in the entire universe contains sentient beings). Contrary, the worst scenario of technological singularity can inflict suffering upon not just 10^{22} existent

---

[107] Tomasik, Brian, How Many Wild Animals Are There?, Essays on Reducing Suffering, http://reducing-suffering.org/how-many-wild-animals-are-there/

sentient beings, but also create more sentient beings to inflict suffering upon. In the case of the damnation, the disutilitarian superintelligence may create 10^30, 10^50 sentient beings to inflict the excruciating suffering upon. Possibly, the disutilitarian AI may create other universes to get energy and material to create sentient beings and inflict suffering upon them. In that case, a disutilitarian AI may create 10^100 (googol), 10^googol (googolplex), 10^googolplex (googolplexplex, googolplexian, googolduplex), googolplexplexplex sentient beings to inflict an immense amount of suffering upon, and so on.

Because a disuitilitarian AI may become able cheat the heat death of the universe (the second law of the thermodynamics) by methods such as a creation of the new universe, a disutilitarian AI may even cause an immense intensity of suffering for an infinite time upon an exponentially increasing number of sentient beings. (for example, the number of victimised sentient beings can be (exponentially) doubled every second, i.e. 1024-folded every 10 seconds, for the infinite duration of the time)

Considering that the damnation of the cosmos might possibly cause the infinite suffering, even if the probability of the infinite suffering happen as a result of technological singularity is one in one billion (10^-9) or one in one googol (10^{-100}), provided that technological singularity can prevent or alleviate only finite suffering, the expected value of the technological singularity under the negative utilitarian view is minus infinite ($-\infty$).

Printed in Great Britain
by Amazon